NOTE *to* SELF

NOTE *to* SELF

ON KEEPING A JOURNAL
AND OTHER DANGEROUS PURSUITS

SAMARA O'SHEA

COLLINS LIVING
An Imprint of HarperCollins Publishers

Grateful acknowledgment is made for permission to quote from the following materials:

From *The Diary of a Young Girl: The Definitive Edition,* by Anne Frank, edited by Otto H. Frank and Mirjam Pressler, translated by Susan Massotty, Copyright © 1995 by Doubleday, a division of Random House, Inc. Used by Permission of Doubleday, a division of Random House, Inc.

From *The Unabridged Journals of Sylvia Plath,* by Sylvia Plath, edited by Karen V. Kukil, copyright © 2000 by the estate of Sylvia Plath. Preface, Notes, Index, Copyright © 2000 by Karen V. Kukil. Used by permission of Anchor Books, a division of Random House, Inc.

Journal entry February 17, 1973, page 8, from the *Journal of Joyce Carol Oates: 1973–1982,* Copyright © 2007 by The Ontario Review, Inc. Reprinted by permission of HarperCollins Publishers.

From *Notebooks* by Tennessee Williams, edited by Margaret Bradham Thornton, Copyright © 2000 by Yale University Press. Reprinted by permission of Yale University Press.

Excerpt from *Incest: From "A Journal of Love,"* by Anaïs Nin, Copyright © 1992 by Rupert Pole, as Trustee under the Last Will and Testament of Anaïs Nin, reproduced by permission of Harcourt, Inc.

HarperCollins books may be purchased for educational, business, or sales promotional use. For information, please write: Special Markets Department, HarperCollins Publishers, 10 East 53rd Street, New York, NY 10022.

FIRST EDITION

Designed by Ralph Fowler / rlf design

The Library of Congress Cataloging-in-Publication Data

O'Shea, Samara.
  Note to self : on keeping a journal and other dangerous pursuits / Samara O'Shea.—1st ed.
    p.   cm.
  1. Diaries—Authorship.   2. Diaries—Authorship   Psychological aspects   I. Title.

  PN4390.O84 2008
808' .06692—dc22

2008005271

ISBN 978-0-06-149415-4

08 09 10 WBC/RRD 10 9 8 7 6 5 4 3 2 1

This book is dedicated to
my distinguished little sister,

Andrea Lynn O'Shea,

the one who has always read my journals
and loved me just the same

NOTE TO READER

REGARDING DATES: My publisher and I decided to move forward with this book by verbal agreement on June 5, 2007. Although I continued to keep a journal beyond that date, there will be no entries found here from after that point, as I feared the knowledge of imminent publication would influence my private writing. Throughout the course of keeping a journal, I dated the majority of my entries. There were, however, a few occasions where I did not, in which case I looked to nearby entries and listed simply the month and the year of the entry.

REGARDING NAMES: Many of the names in this book have been changed and a few of them remain intact. There is no indication as to which is which, to protect the privacy of those who were comfortable having their actual names appear, but who still didn't care to call direct attention to themselves. The names I have changed will remain consistent throughout the book. For example, if someone named Charlie appears in chapter 2 and then again in chapter 5, know that it is the same person I'm referring to. When initials appear in lieu of a name, they are the actual initials of the person being written about.

REGARDING EDITS: I have made some edits to the journal entries, mostly spelling and occasionally grammar. I have only corrected grammar for clarification's sake (and spelling for embarrassment's sake). If the initial grammar in the journal was incorrect but the statement read clearly, then it was left as originally written.

CONTENTS

CHAPTER 11

INTIMATE DETAILS   139

INTRODUCTION:

WRITE FOR YOUR LIFE

We write to taste life twice,
in the moment and in retrospection.

—Anaïs Nin

"I swear to God, this is different."

"You do realize this is the third girl you've said that about," I shot at him curtly—realizing right away how inappropriately callous my tone of voice had become, considering I was dealing with a friend and his broken heart. I tried to quell my frustration. I felt bad that I had allowed myself to become frustrated at all. He had come to me in emotional agony; I was happy to listen and offer advice if I could. I bit my tongue every time it moved to say "Everything happens for a reason." Although I believe it's true, I know it's the last thing anyone wants to hear when a relationship goes sour or when a car gets towed.

His request was straightforward and simple: He wanted to know *why*. I explained gently that I didn't think it was a good idea to continue prompting this woman with that question, because she wasn't going to give him the explanation he craved. Most people are never going to (or usually won't) tell you exactly why, and, also, by asking them, you're making it too important—like your own self-worth depends entirely on their answer. I told my friend this just to say I said it, but it didn't bother me when he reiterated that he still needed to ask. I understood that. I can count plenty of times when my friends were advising me against calling, e-mailing, or approaching a guy who had made it clear he was already out the door, and I said, "Whatever, I'm doing it." My heart overruled my head, and I just needed to know *why*. It is a need both dangerous and pressing. I have since learned it's best to mourn in private, do lots of yoga, and move on.

My friend had yet to master the art of rejection. His desire to dissect the situation didn't bother me—again I've been there—nor did his futile need to contact this woman one final time. My frustration entered stage left when I was referencing his last broken heart (six months prior) and I made some poignant—or so I thought—parallels. He wouldn't have it. He kept insisting that the pain was somehow sharper and his restlessness more stirring this time around. This isn't to say that one broken heart can't outweigh another. Of course, it can. But I'd stood on the sidelines for both of these (all three of them if you count the girl before that). The similarities were striking. His case of emotional amnesia was getting to me, but he was so hurt after my initial offhand comment, I swallowed the aggravation and said calmly, "Will you please write this down? Write it down, so the next time it happens, you can refer to yourself." Because, God knows, he wouldn't believe me.

My piece of advice caught me off guard. I wasn't sure what compelled me to put it that way. Maybe it was because I was at my desk with my shelf full of journals in front of me or because just that morning, I had come across an article that said journaling not only helps one overcome emotional trauma but also strengthens the immune system. I had a proud moment when I read that. I thought if that's true, my immune system must be a small fortress because I've kept journals since I was fifteen *and* I drink insane amounts of green tea. His response to my suggestion was along the lines of "Yeah, yeah. I'll be fine." We both got off the phone feeling defeated. He still suffering, and I wishing I could airlift him from the barren I'll-never-find-another-her desert to the land of good and plenty or milk and honey or beer and babes—whichever he preferred.

Long after our conversation ended, I realized I'd shared the wrong benefit of journaling with him. It's not in the rereading where one finds solace but in the writing itself. It's like crying—you don't know why, but you feel so much better afterward. Everything pours, streams, flows, out of you aimlessly. Afterward, you get to see what your thoughts look like, if you want. You could also just take the emotional-cascade part of the process for what it's worth. And the journal, unlike the less-than-perfect friend, won't get frustrated. As a wise thirteen-year-old named Anne Frank once noted, "Paper has more patience than people." The journal is the (much cheaper) therapist, who isn't hired to tell you what to do but rather to guide you into speaking and speaking (writing and writing) until at last you hear yourself. It's only when you recognize your own problems that you can come to your own solutions.

I first gave journaling a go when I was in elementary school, when it was called a diary. I had several of them, little books with locks on them. One stands out especially—it was royal blue with a gold border and a strong lock. I remember thinking it was too sophisticated to write in, but I got over that. I'm sure it didn't last very many entries. They never did. My first diary horror show took place in the fifth grade. It was the first diary I had that wasn't 5×7. It probably couldn't even be considered a diary—it was one of my mom's notebooks with big binder clips that you put as much or as little paper in as you wanted. I liked it because the pages were big and easier to write on. I told this book all about my big crush on Jason Cusack and about my new friend, Heather Wall. I invited Heather to sleep over one night and was very excited that she was sleeping at my house and not Melissa's. Ah, the little things. Heather was a hyper one and I was much more subdued, so as the night wore on, I grew tired and she became increasingly giddy and I wasn't sure what to do. At one point, she went into the bathroom, and I pulled out my diary and furiously wrote that Heather was getting on my nerves. I put it back beneath my bed before she saw me, or so I thought.

I'm not exactly sure what happened next. Either she asked for something to eat or drink, from downstairs, or I went downstairs for a reason all my own. What I remember clearly is coming back upstairs and being locked out of my room and having her read my diary to me through the door. With every ounce of energy I had stored in my prepubescent body, I banged on that door and shouted with utmost fury. This is what you do when you life had ended. She was reading—barely, as she was laughing so hard—the passage about Jason Cusack. That was the gold she she'd gone digging for. She didn't seem to care that I'd written she was getting on my nerves. I think she was proud of it. Again, my memory fails me, as I don't remember how we got through the rest of the night or how I could stand having her in my house or if I even bothered to ask her meekly not to tell anyone. I'm sure I knew even then that it was pointless. When she left, I not only cried, but I sat in my closet and cried. I needed to be surrounded by darkness and get comfortable in my social grave.

As predicted, she told everyone on Monday morning. She and I were both on the safety patrol, and I can easily conjure the image of her shouting (with deliberate intent to mortify) from her post as I walked to mine. I had no idea what she was saying, but I didn't need to. Walking into class was fun, lots of snickering. The one person who looked at me with understanding and sympathy was Jason Cusack himself. He was neither cocky nor rude; he gave me half a smile as if to say we were on the same side. And we were. Heather had just embarrassed the hell out of him, too. Surprisingly, that didn't discourage me altogether from writing in my diary. I still wrote in it occasionally *and* Heather found it two more times. I didn't care about those times quite as much and am now wondering why I didn't put more thought into a hiding place. (Maybe I subconsciously wanted her to read it.) If you're wondering why I remained friends with her, it was because I wasn't popular enough to have a choice.

I don't have that makeshift diary or any of the earlier ones anymore. I'm sure I didn't see the value in holding on to them. I started writing consistently again when I was in high school, and by that time, I had graduated to calling them journals—there was really no graduation involved, but it sounded more mature to me. I don't recall if I had a motivation for writing; I just did it. My journal was a place to record events and let out whatever needed to be, which can be a lot when you're a teenager.

I do, however, recall placing much more importance on my college journals. The young woman in me started asking herself a lot of questions and trying to figure out the inner workings of her mind. The sexual being wrote of her many cravings, curiosities, and experimentations. The basket case said all the things she was afraid to say elsewhere. And the growing writer in me ran amok. She had a blast playing with words and ignoring the conventions of grammar. For example, at the age of nineteen, I wrote, "My mortality has come un-tethered. To rule the world is my only confection and passion." Let's ignore (if you possibly can) my desire to rule the world and zero in on the word *confection*. I remember reading it in the book *Grace*, by Robert Lacey (a biography of Grace Kelly). I had probably encountered the word before but not in this way—the author of the book kept referring to Grace herself as a confection. I loved it! I loved playing with the meaning of words like that. A confection is "a sweet preparation, such as candy," and referring to a beautiful woman in that way made perfect, breathtaking sense to me. I didn't have as much luck using the word in a clever way, but I certainly kept trying. On February 19, 1999, I wrote, "In a whisper in a whirl I am considered a mess. I want confections to come my way." It kind of makes sense there, but a few days later, on February 26, I lost the meaning again: "I want to conquer sex. I want it to be the pleasure, control, and confection that allows me to be a woman." So there, you now know that at the age of nineteen, I liked the word *confection* enough to use it out of context, and that I wanted to conquer both the world and sex. I have since conquered neither, but I promise to talk about both. The point is, the benefits of a journal became clear to me—it was a place to check in with myself. On those private pages, mind met matter, poetry met prose, and nobody was grading.

I'll tell you up front a journal isn't a road map. It can't be. A journal, rather, is the path of pebbles you leave behind you, so you have the security of knowing you can always return to where you've been. You can re-attempt an obstacle course that kicked your ass the first time. You can run back and apologize to the people you hurt along the way. You can also confront the people who hurt you. You can stand at the mouth of a chasm that separates what you once believed from what you now believe. Or you can keep moving forward, with specific Sodom and Gomorrah–type instructions for yourself never to turn around, knowing the purpose of the journal was for momentary release.

Many of my journal passages were meant only for the moment, in that I now have no idea what I was talking about. On January 2, 1999 ('99 was an enlightening year for me, which is why I keep referring to it, but I promise to unlock the other journals as well), I wrote, "Instead of going outside and gathering men for my army, I stayed inside and thought of you. I suppose it was lazy of me, but it helped me put you in perspective. And now you have my admiration." Yeah. Not a clue. No idea who "you" was or what I thought I needed an army for. I get a kick out of reading it, though, because it's as if someone else wrote it. I suppose someone else did write it. My nineteen-year-old self wrote it, and I don't know her so well anymore. There's a thought! Putting all the girls who wrote these journals in the same room together. If the sweet sixteen-year-old who swore she'd never try drugs and would remain a virgin until marriage mistakenly got her hands on the written ramblings of the unruly twenty-two-year-old, she'd discover that she was destined to break both of those rules—often at the same time. At some point, she'd lift her sad eyes from the pages and innocently ask, "What does blowing lines mean?"

Then the responsible twenty-five-year-old would tap twenty-two on the shoulder and say, "I think you've had enough." Twenty-two would say, "Mind your own business!" She was feisty. I would have to come in and break it up—me, the twenty-eight-year-old matron who oversees them all (my thirty-five-year-old self is rolling her eyes at me; I can feel it.)

Sorry to go schizo on you, but I am amused by my other selves, as I believe everyone should be. We aren't meant to be proud of everything we've done, but we are meant to keep learning and growing. I've found keeping a journal to be a very efficient way of doing that. The older I get, the more I see people who don't know themselves very well. It's a great paradox, not knowing yourself, but it's very real. I see people going through the motions of marriage or of this job or that job all because they think it's what they should do, and they've never bothered to ask themselves what they want to do. My friend with back-to-back broken hearts was being very true to himself in pursuing each girl, so I think journaling would serve a different function for him. It would teach him to recognize his own limits and help him practice some self-discipline. Not that reading a previous journal entry can necessarily dull your present pain, but it can serve as a reminder that you did survive this once before. You end up being your own support system.

As I said, I've kept journals for over ten years through what was a crucial growing period—the latter half of high school, college, and my early twenties. I'd like to share with you not only many of the entries themselves but the stories that surround them, and how journaling has come through for me again and again. I do this with the hope that you might consider embarking on a personal journey of this sort, and if you are already an enthusiastic journaler, then let's compare notes. I do this not because my life is grand or even out of the ordinary. Not to show off. Not even to kiss and tell (although that's inevitable). I do it for the sake of a frame of reference. I'm willing to bet that some of my thoughts and experiences match yours.

I count among the most wonderful moments we can experience as human beings those in which we're walking around thinking we're the only ones. *I'm the only one who's ever done this dumb thing. I'm the only one who's ever had this random set of feelings. I'm the only one who's ever suffered in such a way.* And then we happen upon a poem or a song, a movie scene, a play, a page in a book, and we see ourselves. It's as if the writer had stolen the thoughts directly from the dusty shelves in our minds or he or she had ripped the seemingly unique events from our vulnerable memories. The writer whispers, "It's okay. Me, too." It is a satisfying moment when you realize you're not the only one who thinks orange juice tastes funny after you brush your teeth. We collectively breathe a sigh of relief when we realize we are not alone in our thoughts, words, or deeds. I don't pretend you'll identify with everything in this book, but if you can identify with something, then I've done my job. Of course, I need to identify with others, too; to that end, I'll share some journal entries and literary passages of those I've identified with and even those I hope never to identify with—sometimes knowing who you are comes from knowing who you aren't. The first sage I give you is Richard Rhodes. In his book *How to Write: Advice and Reflections,* he captures soulfully the inherent value of the act of writing. "The process of writing is always a healing process because the function of creation is always, *always*, the alleviation of pain—the writer's first of all and then the pain of those who read what she has written. Imagination is compassionate. Writing is a form of making, and making humanizes the world."

❋ ❋ ❋

CHAPTER 1

IN THE BEGINNING

In the beginning was the Word . . .

—John 1:1

I think we all know or know someone who knows that person—the person who keeps a daily, very meticulous diary. They end each day with a cup of tea or perhaps a scotch on the rocks. They sit in a large velvet armchair and pull out a black leather hardcover journal with their name imprinted on it—very *Masterpiece Theatre*. Then with a majestic black fountain pen poised over a blank page, they relax and write. They record the day's events in the order that they happened, and they do this devotedly each night before bed.

I don't mean to criticize daily diarists. I envy them—I wish I had that sort of self-discipline, and I also wish I could drink straight scotch. However, it's the knowledge of this methodical type of journaling that often prevents the rest of us from even attempting to keep a journal. I tried to start several journals as an adolescent and I would get so frustrated with myself if I (1) didn't write every day and (2) left out anything that happened during the day. None of these journals ever got off the ground. I finally got the journal thing going when I took both of those pressures off myself. I changed the rules: Write when you want and write whatever you want. I was fifteen at the time, and I now have eleven journals to show for lifting that lid of ridiculous expectation off myself.

A journal is one of the only places where no one can judge you, and it should also be a place where you are not judging yourself. It's difficult to do that when you're already criticizing yourself for falling short of the process, so I invite you to dismiss everything you think a journal should be from your mind. Your journal is an extension of you, and therefore it can be whatever you want it to be. You can write every day or once a year. It can be a place to write one word to describe a feeling or event, a place where you emote in endless paragraphs without any punctuation, a place where you write upside down and backward, a place where you start your own language. Whether it's all of the above or none of the above, the purpose of your journal is to serve as a mirror for your mind. You are your own universe. Your mind is vast, and even you can't know of all the passions, insights, fears, and troubles that dwell within. A journal is an effective way to peel back the fleshy onion layers and get to the center of yourself—bear in mind that there can be tears involved when handling an onion.

You may be thinking, *But I'm not a writer!* If you're a thinker, then you're a writer, for writing is simply thoughts making their way to paper. Don't be self-conscious about your style or your approach. Remember, the point of the journal is to temporarily eliminate self-consciousness. Don't worry about grammar, spelling, or the morality factor of your words and deeds. Put whatever is swirling around in the back of your brain on the page and see what it looks like. Or don't. Maybe you'll write it and throw it away immediately. But if a thought is begging to breathe the fresh air, then it's best to open the door and let it out.

I have watched my thoughts—some mundane, others vibrant and strange—make their way to paper countless times and in a variety of ways. My journal has been the looking glass I've held up to myself on numerous occasions; some days I like the reflection and other days I am certain that a more hideous, uninteresting ogre has never existed. My diary has helped me gain an understanding of who I am, what I want out of life, and how to apply superglue when things don't go my way. I put forth the disclaimer that life is an onward, upward climb and I am far from knowing everything—even about myself. I have learned, however, that life may not be about knowing everything, but it is about taking the limited knowledge and experience that we have and making that work for us. It's being able to live our lives in such a way that we don't feel we're missing out on anything and also being able to stand still and strong in the middle of unexpected storms. I gladly share with you the methods of my journal madness. Please know that everything I offer is a suggestion, and that there is no right or wrong way to keep a journal.

THE FIRST PAGE

I've always felt a pressure to be profound on the first page of a new journal. I won't say that I always achieve profundity, but I do try. Since there is no obvious outside source creating this pressure, I imagine it's one I put on myself: *Say something smart to look back on later!* I prefer to think it's nothing like that, but more like the beginning of anything. A new year. A new job. A new relationship. All of these, essentially, are the start of new seasons in our lives, and we want them to be as fresh as clean linens drying in the path of a friendly breeze. So we show off a bit at first—doing everything as diligently as possible. Going to the gym every day, showing up a half hour early for work, or tending to a new lover as if he or she were royalty. In the same vein, we start our journals off on a semi-philosophical note, or at least we acknowledge the fresh start we feel we're making with our words and the act of journaling itself.

There is also the possibility that "that future person," as my mother refers to the unknown individual who might read through all of one's journals someday, is putting the pressure on me from a date that has yet to come. Most of us can't help but think it's possible that a curious pass-erby will someday indulge in our journals (in my mother's case, that person will mostly likely be me). This idea thrills many, while others wouldn't mind only as long as they were dead, and still others are horri-fied at the thought and would burn their journals before they allowed them to fall into wayward hands. I clearly don't mind opening my jour-nal for outside eyes to see, and the reason is that, in a way, I am dead. Well, I'm not dead, but these written versions of me are. They came (I'm glad they did), had their great moments, made their great mistakes, and went away. All that's left of them now are these journal entries and plenty of bad photos. In some cases, I have things in common with the girls who wrote these entries, while in others, I don't identify at all.

Not everyone suffers from "first-page pressure"; my mother had no idea what I was talking about when I asked her if she'd ever felt it. She says she just picks up a new journal and starts where she left off with the old one. Alas, I do suffer from it, and just as New Year's resolutions slip away, a new job becomes routine, and relationships hit a brick wall of banality, I even-tually stop writing my journal for that future person and write just for me. My handwriting eventually starts to slip as well. Yet with every new blank book I purchase, I circle back and enjoy a fresh start all over again.

The following are a few of my first-page entries from over the years. I realized as I put them side by side (a notably odd experience) that most of them were written for that future person. In almost all of them, I felt the need to state my age (as if I couldn't figure it out by the date) or declare something I'm sure I thought was wise at the time. There is a different event driving each entry—a fear I had to have my life together the day I graduated college, the death of my grandmom, an early inclination to-ward love—but for the most part, a "new beginning" or "here's where my life is" theme permeates.

AT SIXTEEN

November 10, 1995

I've never suffered from apathy. My problem is that my emotions are too strong and uncontrollable. I'm sixteen years old but I feel about eight. The world around me is foreign and I'll never understand it. People and their actions are so weird. At this point in time I do in fact have a boyfriend. The best part is I actually like him. I'm not yet completely infatuated but I hope that'll change. He's unlike anyone I've ever been attracted to before. He's smart enough to be an honor student but he settles for second best. He's an excellent artist (I have this thing for artists). He's a Christian but in a different way. Revelation is his favorite book [in the Bible] and he analyzes every detail. He's done every drug except for crack and heroin. That excites me so much because I know I'll never do any drug so he's my link to an unknown world. He's been clean for three months now. I want to know what goes on in his head. I pray the Lord's hand will be upon this relationship and everything will work out.

AT NINETEEN

March 27, 1999

I adore the smell of a blank book—so many stories waiting for their turn to be written. I've started at least six journals in my life and each time I do I feel the same array of sickening emotions. Will my words ever matter to others? Will I ever be an accomplished individual?

My 2nd year of college but first year at Duquesne is closing in on me. I enjoy the warm weather immensely but the warmer it becomes the more I fear. Because that means graduation is upon us. Well, upon the seniors. I've met a handful of seniors this year and I know some will go, never to be seen again by me. I fear good-byes and life is filled with constant good-byes. Once the seniors have left then that leaves me with only two years to get my life together. All these thoughts make me anxious and my passions stir as if in a baker's vat. I am hoping to compose myself and live out the remainder of the semester with attractive dignity.

I have gotten myself into a great deal of trouble this semester. Trouble with boys and feelings. But I suppose this is normal for a naïve college girl. I hope to take these troubles and turn them into lessons. I hope to take these lessons and live an optimistic but aware lifestyle. I hope to discern myself with the beauty of kindness, language, and human passions.

I let go of 16 faster than I should have. I'm determined to hold on to 19, but I'm not sure how. Can I make the days last longer than they do? Can I wrap minutes around me like a homemade quilt? Can I leave a lasting impression on those I meet? Can I allow them to make a lasting impression on me?

AT TWENTY-ONE

January 20, 2001

This inclination is strong.* As strong as the wind waking up the ocean water. It hasn't been this strong in almost a year. My God! A Year! Another year has gone by, and at the anxious age of 21 I'm starting to feel the years. The years haven't gotten to me yet, but I feel them nonetheless.

Perhaps it was my grandmom who whispered to me that I couldn't stop writing. I don't remember her saying anything of the sort but perhaps she did. I saw her tonight. I saw her for what may very well be the last time. At the wrinkled age of 86 she is the victim of a very

---

*I'm talking about the inclination to write.

aggressive liver cancer. Looking at her today was strange. She was tethered in 1,000 tubes and her soft, toothless mouth could barely bring thought to the surface. I kept thinking, "All human things are subject to decay."* Not the most respectful thought, I know. But I thanked her for taking such good care of me. She took my hand and raised it to her raisin-wrinkled mouth and kissed it. Probably the nicest moment we've shared in years. I tried to cry softly enough so she couldn't tell. Then I told her how proud I was and how in love with her I was. Now, I hope to hold that moment close. Forever.

January 21, 2001

[This is actually a second-page entry, but it captures the fascination that sometimes comes with a new journal.]

A new journal requires the same mindless yet constant passion of a new lover. It's my guess that I'll pull this little darling out every 3 hours for the next two weeks. Well, maybe not, but I'll think about it.

AT TWENTY-FOUR

December 1, 2003
Fascinating, beautiful blank pages, I have come to fill you! I finished my last journal yesterday and was anxious to begin a new one even then. Today—after a fun lunch with Zazel and Lisa—I stopped by the church to pick up a pie I bought from the boys' choir. The sky was a gorgeous gray and the wind was in upheaval. My hair must have looked like the snakes of Medusa as it twirled about, and I couldn't seem to situate myself, the

---

*This is the opening line from a John Dryden (1621–1700) poem entitled "Mac Flecknoe": "All human things are subject to decay, / And, when Fate summons, monarchs must obey."

pie box, and my purse into adequate walking positions. I made it to the corner of 17th and Irving when my thoughts set sail. I thought of Tyler and the ways in which he's elated me and I had given myself an assignment yesterday—to record with utmost accuracy the dealings involved when falling in love. I can say with a buttery tingle in my stomach that I am going to fall in love with Tyler. If he doesn't push me away and interrupt the procedure then I'm his. I adore him with a childish fervor. There is unprecedented pleasure in sex with him and riding beside him in the car. Getting to know him is sweet and savory. He is both a precious memory and a current issue. I can feel it coming and I want to document the fall. From leap to plunge or push to plunge. I want to write all of it.

Anyway, I decided this on the corner of 17th and Irving so I went right to Barnes & Noble to purchase this journal. I wanted to begin. I want to define the "you just know" feeling. My first find is comfort. In Tyler's presence I am nervous but the comfort rises and I know through his tender gestures I can relax.

FYI: Unfortunately, he does interrupt the process (stupid boy!). In my very next journal entry (December 3), I lament that I hadn't heard from him in two days. By December 14, my heart was good and broken. For the continuing saga, see Chapter 3, "Hearts that Hurt," on page 32.

AT TWENTY-FIVE

September 24, 2004

My sweet Elise gave me this journal today so that I could begin my 25th year armed with a pen and a book in which to tell my story. New beginnings never get old. I've had a wonderful week celebrating my birthday with friends. I am now in Penn Station waiting for my darling cousin Kate so that we may go home and have one final celebration with my family. The fall equinox came as scheduled and brought with her the velvet weather. The sounds and smells of a new season. A new beginning.

EXPRESS YOURSELF, DON'T REPRESS YOURSELF

A good friend of mine and I were discussing the therapy factor in reading other people's journals. There is personal substantiation in seeing your own strange thoughts exhibited in someone else's cerebral showcase. She asked, "Does that make it okay for me to write *everything* I think about in my journal—because I think about killing people sometimes." I can say with a degree of certainty that my friend's journal would not, could not, resemble Charles Manson's. However, I'm sure the thought of handing her ex-boyfriend's new girlfriend a whiskey sour with a dash of cyanide in it has occurred to her. To that, I say, "Write away!"

Writing solidifies thought, which can be unnerving, but it also gives you a sense of control. Maybe the risky notion just needs to be written to be released. Perhaps seeing it will enable you to recognize its ridiculousness, or maybe you'll have to write it many times for that to take place. Writing also makes thoughts easier to deal with or at least to acknowledge, which is the first step in just about anything. You need to acknowledge a dream before you can pursue it. You need to acknowledge a problem before it can be solved. You need to acknowledge pain before healing can begin. I've found that the acknowledgment part is sometimes harder than whatever needs to come after it. The thing not to do is to tell yourself, *I'm not thinking that thought. Who thinks an absurd thought like that?* We all do. We all have moments of madness, and the more in tune you are with all of your thoughts—even the ones you'd rather not have—the more in tune you are with yourself. This isn't to say that all thoughts worth recording need to be inappropriate or frightening. Recording blissful thoughts and experiences is important, too. You can relive the happiness as you write and then again later as you read.

- **Say Anything:** We all have an idea of what a journal should be—whether it's a simple daily record or something only teenage girls have—but there are no *shoulds* here, only *woulds*. Make your journal what you would have it be. I mean it when I say write the good, bad, mad, angry, boring, and ugly. It can be any length and can address any topic. You can write in the first, second, or third person. You can write about your current feelings, yesterday's feelings, the events of the day, the events you wished had taken place, a Shakespearean sonnet, or an anti–Shakespearean sonnet. This is more difficult than it sounds—writing in an unruly way—but it is very liberating.

- **Instant Gratification:** In our preprogrammed world of fast food and faster communications, we tend to like our results right now. This may or may not happen with your journal. Sometimes, a writing session will be the fast-acting mental medicine needed to release pent-up emotions, and other times, it will just be the beginning of getting to know yourself or dealing with a problem. Don't lose all faith if you don't feel ten times better after writing. The long-term effects of a journal are having a record of your life and being able to track your emotional evolution. Each entry will play a part in the grand scheme of your journal, and you will reveal things to yourself whether it's right away or over the course of time.

- **Getting Started:** You don't have to decide what type of diarist you want to be. Simply start writing and your journal will take on a life of its own. If there's nothing pressing on your mind when you begin to write, you can start by asking yourself a question or explaining something to yourself. For example:

Ask Yourself

- How am I feeling?
- How do I want to be feeling?
- What do I want to accomplish today?
- What went wrong today?
- What went right today?
- What role do I want my journal to play in my life?
- What do I want to learn about myself?
- What do I want to change about myself?
- What would I never change about myself?

Tell Yourself

- Describe the room.
- Describe the people in the room.
- Describe the people in your life.
- Describe yourself.
- Describe the aspects of your life that you're pleased with and those areas you're displeased with.
- Describe something you have done many times but have never written about, such as eating ice cream or exercising.

THE DIARY VERSUS JOURNAL DILEMMA

Before you worry about your first entry, you might like to know if you're contributing to a diary or a journal. I wish I could tell you. That's been up in the air for a while—Wikipedia even has an entire page dedicated to the difference. Let's see what they have to say:

> Some use the words "diary" and "journal" interchangeably, while others apply strict differences to journals, diaries and the practice of journaling (dated vs. undated, inner focused vs. outer focused, sporadic entries vs. regular entries, etc.). While traditionalists prefer the use of the term "diary," the current preference (based on book and article titles) is to use the word "journal."

Hmm, I'm a dated/inner-focused/sporadic-entry kind of gal (who likes long walks on the beach), but I still don't know if I keep a diary or a journal. I do know that I am not a traditionalist—therefore I feel no obligation to use the term *diary*. At one point in college, I made my own personal distinction between the two. A diary to me was a basic record of the day's events. Something like "Got up. Brushed teeth. Drank a glass of milk before heading to rugby practice." And a journal was more of an emotional log. As in "The morning's milk was as sour as my mood, which I knew would make me the manly monster not to be messed with at rugby practice." I also associated diaries with teenagers and journals with adults. I did away with my distinction when I started encountering and caring about published journals/diaries. For example, *The Diary of Anaïs Nin* is just as emotionally gripping as *The Grand Surprise: The Journals of Leo Lerman*. I could throw you a total loop and tell you that Tennessee Williams's collection of diary/journal entries is simply entitled *Notebooks*, but I won't.

Luckily, this debate is not nearly as big of a deal as who killed Kennedy or whether or not Lindsay Lohan's boobs are real, and therefore I am completely comfortable declaring that a diary, a journal, and a notebook are now and will continue to be interchangeable on every page throughout this book.

RED LIGHT/GREEN LIGHT JOURNALS

I was journaling in the dark a few weeks ago with only the light of my laptop to guide me. I do that for no good reason sometimes. My sister stuck her head in the room and asked (as anyone would), "Don't you want some light?" Before I answered, she said, "I didn't get that gene!" I knew exactly what she was talking about—she meant the journaling gene. My mother and I are avid diarists, but it's not something my sister has ever really taken to, though she's tried many times. As the universe would have it, I found one of her few journals the next day as I was going through boxes in the basement. It only had twelve pages of writing in it. I read and laughed at every entry.

I'm sure you're thinking I had no business reading what she wrote. Normally that is the case, but not here. My sister and I have always (I'm guessing will always) read each other's journals. I'd come home from college and we'd settle down in her room with a bowl of popcorn and exchange books. Mine were always store-bought journals, and she usually used wire-bound notebooks. We laughed most of the time, but there were a few entries that yielded a more pensive "Oh, I'm so sorry he did that" reply. She would pick up on sentences I hadn't thought twice about and howl at things I hadn't found remotely funny, and I would do the same for her. Our insights into each other's insights were (what's the word I'm looking for?) insightful. That was my sister's most productive time as a "journalist"; she was in high school, and she's only attempted one journal since then, during her senior year of college. It was that senior-year journal that I found.

Now (oh my, it's taken me a long time to get to the point), if you are like my sister in that you start journals with great excitement, write several eager entries, and then neglect them sooner than later, who cares? Don't let yourself be discouraged because you stop and go. Red light. Green light. Red light again. If you write entries every January 1, 2, and 3, then inevitably lose your journal in the hamper, give yourself the green light to write your standard three entries again next year—knowing it mostly likely won't go any further than that. It's better than nothing. You will come across those half-written, quarter-written, half-page entries, and, as with all diaries, you are guaranteed to get a kick out of yourself. If you'd never go so far as to even purchase a journal because you know it'll just sit on your shelf, consider some random journaling. If you have an afternoon epiphany, an emotional earthquake, or a bizarre thought, see what it looks like on the nearest piece of paper—napkin, notebook, envelope. Then shove it somewhere like the back of a book or a desk drawer. It'll pop up again, I promise.

If you're all-tech-all-the-time and refuse to write anything by hand, then I recommend keeping a folder on your desktop for accidental musings. There is software designed just for journaling. Sorry, I can't tell you more than that—I'm a die-hard, hands-on kind of journaler. I do advise against entering these into your cell phone or BlackBerry—they run a greater risk of disappearing for good.

Here is the first entry of my sister's last makeshift journal (or diary, as she clearly calls it). This only lived through seven entries.

January 5, 2003

Dear Diary,

Well, my New Year's resolution is to write more. Write more poems, write a novel, and keep a regular diary. Why? Because I know I can do it.

I know I'm a good writer and I have visions of grandeur floating around in my head. I guess it's not enough that I know I can do it. I want other people to say, "Damn that's good!" Why I want that I can't say →
which I guess is why I need this diary, to figure myself out. I'm hoping when I come back and read this in 2004 I won't tear the pages out like I've done to other diaries. But anyway I'll just dive in and talk about the juicy stuff.

André. I am madly in love with him. That gets reaffirmed whenever I read the notes he leaves for me, or just when I look into his (beautiful brown) eyes. But lately we've been fighting. I don't really know about what. I get pissed off by the way he treats me sometimes. He'll talk to me like I'm a child. He says it's just "his way." Well what the fuck am I supposed to do with that? I look at everything in the sense of eternity, and sometimes I'm sure he is my eternity and sometimes I'm sure he's not.

The other day when we fought I told him that I think his issues are all spawned from his sister. He actually agreed with me! How unfair is that though. And how do I deal with this? I can't hate her if I'm telling him to forgive her, but how do you not dislike someone so two faced? That conversation gave way to the idea for my book, so I guess when I do write it and if it goes anywhere, I'll owe part of it to her. There's a scary thought! More later.

ANNE FRANK (1929–1945) ON WRITING THE FIRST FEW ENTRIES IN YOUR NEW DIARY

I have a confession: Up until this point I have never read Anne Frank's diary. I can think of a few times I've thumbed through it, and I've always loved the idea of it—of her sweet musings being an innocent, optimistic testimony to a tragic circumstance. How do I say this? I. Had. No. Idea. I am and will continue to be beside myself at how astute she was. She had a remarkable sense of self at an unheard of age. She offered compelling insight into the adult mingling going on around her, while still recording the natural curiosities of any teenager. Anne begins writing the day she turns thirteen, just after receiving the diary as a gift. In these first few entries, she writes of having a diary for the first time in her life and goes on to give the book the name Kitty. She also explains, quite thoroughly, the role she hopes the diary will play in her life.

June 12, 1942
(Anne's thirteenth birthday)

I hope I will be able to confide everything to you, as I have never been able to confide in anyone, and I hope you will be a great source of comfort and support.

Sunday, June 14, 1942

I'll begin from the moment I got you, the moment I saw you lying on the table among my other birthday presents. (I went along when you were bought but that doesn't count.) One Friday June 12, I was awake at six o'clock, which isn't surprising, since it was my birthday. But I'm not allowed to get up at that hour, so I had to control my curiosity until quarter to seven. When I couldn't wait any longer, I went to the dining room, where Moortje (the cat) welcomed me by rubbing against my legs.

    A little after seven I went to Daddy and Mama and then to the living room to open my presents, and you were the first thing I saw, maybe one of my nicest presents. Then a bouquet of roses, some peonies, and a potted plant. From Daddy and Mama I got a blue blouse, a game, a bottle of grape juice, which to my mind tasted a bit like wine (after all, wine is made from grapes), a puzzle, a jar of cold cream, 2.50 guilders and a gift certificate for two books. I got another book as well, Camera Obscura (but Margot already has it, so I exchanged mine for something else), a platter of homemade cookies (which I made myself, of course, since I've become quite an expert at baking cookies), lots of candy and a strawberry tart from Mother. And a letter from Granny, right on time, but of course that was just a coincidence. . . .

Saturday, June 20, 1942

Writing in a diary is a really strange experience for someone like me. Not only because I've never written anything before, but also because it seems to me that later on neither I nor anyone else will be interested in the musings of a thirteen-year-old schoolgirl. Oh well, it doesn't matter. I feel like writing, and I have an even greater need to get all kinds of things off my chest.

"Paper has more patience than people." I thought of this saying on one of those days when I was feeling a little depressed and was sitting at home with my chin in my hands, bored and listless, wondering whether to stay in or go out. I finally stayed where I was, brooding. Yes, paper does have more patience, and since I'm not planning to let anyone else read this stiff-backed notebook grandly referred to as a "diary," unless I should ever find a real friend, it probably won't make a bit of difference. Now I'm back to the point that prompted me to keep a diary in the first place: I don't have a friend.

Let me put it more clearly, since no one will believe that a thirteen-year-old girl is completely alone in the world. And I'm not. I have loving parents and a sixteen-year-old sister, and there are about thirty people I can call friends. I have a throng of admirers who can't keep their adoring eyes off me and who sometimes resort to using a broken pocket mirror to try and catch a glimpse of me in the classroom.

I have a family, loving aunts and uncles and a good home. No, on the surface I seem to have everything, except my one true friend. All I think about when I'm with friends is having a good time. I can't bring myself to talk about anything but ordinary everyday things. We don't seem to be able to get any closer, and that's the problem. Maybe it's my fault that we don't confide in each other. In any case, that's just how things are, and unfortunately they're not liable to change. This is why I've started a diary.

To enhance the image of my long-awaited friend in my imagination, I don't just want to jot down the facts in a diary the way most people would do, but I want the diary to be my friend, and I'm going to call this friend Kitty. . . .

✳ ✳ ✳

ROMANCE ON RECORD

Well, my heart knows me better than I know myself,
so I'm gonna let it do all the talking.

—KT Tunstall

I was on the phone with a friend the other day and when the topic of journals came up, she confessed, "I haven't written in mine in a while because I just haven't been happy." I responded in bewilderment, "You mean you write in your journal more often when you're happy?"

"Yeah, when do you write in it?"

"When I'm sad."

"Oh, isn't that interesting. I don't write when I'm sad."

I had never met someone, knowingly anyway, who turned to their journal primarily in moments of joy. I thought it was wonderful that happiness inspired my friend to write, and I naturally felt bad that she hadn't written in a while. For most of my life, it's been the opposite, and I've turned to my journal in the name of misery more than anything else. Nowadays, I make a conscious effort to see that each of my emotions receives more playing time on the page, because I'm not as troubled as I once was (can I get a cheesy double thumbs up?), but there was a time—in the age of teenage angst and college drama—when sorrowful emotions and fears cast their distressing shadows all over my journal. At nineteen, I wrote a journal-message to my boyfriend about this:

October 11, 1999

Jesse, I'm writing this for you in case you ever find yourself thumbing through my journal. You may be angry at this point because your name has not been mentioned, but there's a simple explanation for that. I spend most of my time writing about people who belittle and degrade me. I know it's absurd, but that's how journals usually work. People like to release negative energy. Seldom do I write my elations because I'm too busy elating.

I apologize for the downer this introduction has been thus far as we move our way into the chapter on love, but I tell you these things so you'll understand why I had to scrounge for love-drunk journal entries. I managed to find a few and, moving forward, my aim is to give love and romance all the written accolades they deserve. It is important to write about infatuation and love, because with the intoxicating sensations that accompany those frames of mind also comes the chance to be innocent and naive at any age. If you're falling for someone new or re-falling for someone old, you surrender your know-how to the powers that be and act like a fool. This is a good thing—we need to get in touch with our inner fool every now and then. Handing a pen and paper to this spellbound version of yourself is guaranteed to amuse. It can also serve as a reminder of your glory days when your relationship needs a pick-me-up. One of the nice things about the early days of love is you feel as if you've never felt this way before. Each new object of affection brings back feelings of spring—a season both very familiar and brand new every time.

Now, I said I had very few lovey-dovey journal entries, but I didn't say there were none. What you are about to read is the crème de la crème—the best love entries my collective journals have to offer. This may not be saying much, but I am glad I have a few accounts of infatuation. Here are the tales of four men who sent me all dreamy-eyed to my diary, because I just *had* to run in and write about them.

AT FIFTEEN

February 12, 1995

I've decided I have a sick mind. Let me start from the beginning. Last Monday Jordan's boyfriend Anthony introduced me to his friend Shawn. He's really cute and sweet but he's not a Christian. He really doesn't care about religion. At first that bothered me. I was afraid of getting to know him. Well, I was wrong.

Friday night he took me to the Mr. Kingsway pageant (it was hilarious). Then he took me to an empty parking lot and let me drive his car. Then we went to an empty playground and sat on the equipment and just talked. Then we went over Misti's house for a while. Then he drove me home at 11 and we just stayed in each other's arms talking for an hour (it was freezing!). But we talked about everything and he told me he wouldn't kiss me because he didn't want to ruin everything. Then when it was time to go inside I kissed him on the cheek. He looked at me and said, "Well, I guess I can have just one." Then he kissed me. He was such a gentleman. I saw him Saturday too. I like him so much. Anyway, as I sleep or daydream I find myself thinking about the things I want us to do. I want him to touch me where it feels good. Just because I don't believe in pre-marital sex doesn't mean I can't think about other *things*. I told him that I don't believe in pre-marital sex and he *doesn't care*.

P.S. Two days till St. Valentine's

December 5, 1995

I finally found a blue pen. Yes! My feelings for Jonathan are growing so strong. He's such a comfort. The sweet things he says are incredible. I love the way he looks at me. Kissing him has become an awesome pleasure. I can't believe he's mine, all mine.

We are the weirdest couple in the world, but that makes it so much fun. To everyone we must look so awkward. I'm taller than he is, not to mention how he was into drugs and I've never even come close to doing them. Yes, we must appear strange, but I think we're adorable. They can think whatever they want.

AT TWENTY

February 6, 2000

Let this day be blest. Let this moment be mine—for after some barren time I am finally inspired to write. I have concentrated solely on Jesse these past few months. I have found him to be the only one who will ever truly satisfy me. He is my perfect companion . . . in conversation . . . in support . . . in compassion . . . in absolute laughter . . . and in honest love. I cling to him without the terrible mystery I find so attractive.

He is precious in my sight and I in his. I made love with my love last night. I ignored all of my experience and did my best to just feel him and his intentions. Afterwards, tears rolled from his eyes like dew dripping from a soft leaf. Precious. It was all too precious. Now, we love each other. We make love. We fuck. We enjoy. And afterwards we fall into each other with happiness and exhaustion.

AT TWENTY-FOUR

November 30, 2003

Well, I'll say one thing for him—he makes me want to write. Makes me want to sift carefully through these feelings that I've felt before—desire, longing, comfort, pleasure, sincerity, curiosity—but I've never felt them in this order and they're being reciprocated which is throwing me completely off. Without knowing it Tyler keeps me guessing constantly but every now and then he turns to me and extends an unexpected compliment or flattering glance. He calms me, he fills me, and he adores me. But I don't know the boundaries of his adoration nor do I know the boundaries of my own. I feel like I could give up New York for him—Sunday afternoons and summers on the beach could make this city a sweet memory. But it's too soon to tell—for now I won't resist plunging into a whirlpool of engaging emotions and I hope I come out clean only to find that I haven't fallen into uncertainty but that I've fallen in love.

EXPRESS YOURSELF
WITH OTHER PEOPLE'S WORDS

There are two times in life—when you're madly in love and when your heart is good and broken—that you'll inadvertently pay more attention to the words around you. Song lyrics stand out and you tend to read quotes plastered on signs and greeting cards more carefully. In the case of love, you want a feel-good song or an old-school poem to verify and heighten the way you feel. In the case of a broken heart, you uncon-sciously look for evidence that other people have been there, too (more on broken hearts in the next chapter).

In the same way you may once have given your sweetie a mixed tape in high school—using other people's words and concepts to express how you felt—you can do the same for yourself in your journal. It sounds con-tradictory, I realize, but writing other people's words in your diary can help you find yourself. When you encounter an article, quote, or poem that moves you, it's because you see your own beliefs, opinions, and expe-riences reflected. Whether it's a personal philosophy you already knew you had or one you're discovering you have, someone else has expressed it well and you feel a connection. Copy down the quotes that move you, because they, in addition to or in lieu of your own words, will testify to how you saw the world at a certain age.

- **Find Purpose in Poetry:** Poetry is something you have to go out of your way to find these days—it was once featured in almost every newsstand publication, and kudos to the publications that still print it. If I do seek it out or happen upon a poem I like, sometimes I'll Xerox it and paste it in my journal. Other times, I'll copy the words myself. Copying the words is another way to experience them. In February 2001, I was one month into my senior year of college when my British literature class was studying Lord Byron's masterpiece poem entitled *Don Juan* (1818). I was stopped in my tracks by a stanza where a female character describes the difference between the way men and women experience love.

"Man's love is of man's life a thing apart,
'Tis woman's whole existence; man may range
The court, camp, church, the vessel, and the mart,
Sword, gown, gain, glory, offer in exchange
Pride, fame, ambition, to fill up his heart,

And few there are whom these can not estrange;
Men have all these resources, we but one,
To love again, and be again undone."

- **Transcribe Song Lyrics:** I've only started copying song lyrics into my journal in recent years. In the wake of a broken heart, I kept the songs "Another Girl's Paradise," by Tori Amos, and "Ain't It Funny," by Jennifer Lopez (she was going by J. Lo on that album), on never-ending replay, so one day, I transcribed the songs' lyrics. As with copying Lord Byron's poem, the act was soothing and enabled me to experience the meaning of both songs on a deeper level.

- **Copy Quotes:** This I have done since my first journal and will do it until my very last, I'm sure. I copy quotes large and small from sages both well known and unknown. If I see something on a billboard or in a book, if I hear one in a movie and it moves my core, then it goes in my journal. Each of my eleven journals has one particular quote as a theme that I write on the inside flap, as well as countless other quotes inside. Rereading my journals and seeing the quotes placed between my entries is remarkable—as they often mirror one another. The quotes you identify with can tell you a lot about the place you're in or tell your future self about the place you were in. Here you'll find many of the quotes found in my journals spread throughout (if a quote doesn't have a date attached to it, that means I sought it out specifically for this book).

"I LOVE YOU, TOO"?

Normally what happens when I read old journal entries, especially those from my teenage years, is I encounter my once ways of thinking.

Adolescent philosophies and fears sit on the page and mock me from the past. They don't mock in a mean way but rather in an *Oh, honey, you have so much to learn* way. (Disclaimer: I'm sure ten years from now I'll be saying that about many of the things I'm writing now.) There is the rare occasion, however, when I read one of my teenage tangents and I couldn't agree more. It's a momentary triumph when that happens, but a triumph nonetheless. I think "Whew! We got *something* right the first time."

One of those time-tested ways of thinking is my theory on saying, or rather not saying, "I love you" just because someone else said it first. When I was a freshman in high school, I had my first long-term (eight months, if I recall) boyfriend. After a few months, he started saying "I love you," and I always said it back, though I knew I didn't mean it. If you pulled me aside at the time and asked me if I meant what I was saying, I would have said, "No, but he says it to me, so I have to say it back." I knew that I wanted to be in love and hoped saying the words would produce the feeling (although doing that conjures as much love as the word *abracadabra* conjures actual magic). After we broke up, I decided that was ridiculous and promised I'd never do it again—even if it was to the detriment of the relationship and disappointment of the other person.

The next time I had a boyfriend—my junior year of high school—that's exactly how it went. He told me he loved me, and I never said it back because I was uncertain and had my sights set on being certain where love was concerned. When I got to college, I warned my boyfriend up front. In the early, very early, days of dating, before "I love you" could even come into play, I told him two things: (1) Never buy me gold jewelry. I hate gold. (2) I believe people should say "I love you" in their own time and that means, sometimes, not saying it back immediately. Within four months, he had spent a lot of money on a large gold shamrock-pendant necklace and was really upset when it took me more than a month to return his first "I love you." So much for being up front. I realize it takes courage to tell someone you love them, and not hearing the words right back can make you feel self-conscious—as if you were a soggy flag flapping in the wind. But if you had to choose between having someone say "I love you, too" just to appease and waiting a while and knowing that when they did say it, it would be backed up with the brazen force of the emotion, then I think you would choose the latter.

This doesn't mean I'm opposed to saying "I love you" first. If I feel it first, then I'll gladly say it first, and my boyfriend is welcome to take his time responding. I waited tables with a girl once who refused to say it until her boyfriend said it first. I always had to walk far away from those conversations because they angered me so much. If you can't say it unless the other person says it, then that means your love is contingent on his or her love, and, despite popular belief, that's not love. This also doesn't mean there's anything wrong with saying "I love you, too," provided you mean just that. Anyway, these are a few of the journal entries that are a testimony to my coming into this way of thinking, written at sixteen:

February 1, 1996

Jonathan dropped me off at home last night and I kissed him and got out of the car. As I went to close the door he said, "I love you, Samara." It took a moment to sink in because he told me he'd never say it unless he meant it. I leaned back into the car and pressed my lips against his. I didn't say it back because I'm not sure if I'm in love and I won't say it unless I know for <u>sure</u> that I mean it. I wasn't expecting it at all, and I was a little upset. I wanted him to say it while looking me in the eyes. But the more I thought about it, the more I realized that it was his time and it was perfect.

February 10, 1996

Last night we went for an exciting ride down Breakneck Road and ended up at Taco Bell. Afterwards we went to Misti's house and played truth or dare. The question "Have you ever been in love?" came up. Everyone answered yes except Mike and Megan, until it was Jonathan's turn to answer. He looked at me and said, "You first." I said I'd never been in love (I wasn't about to lie). Then Jonathan said he's never been in love either. But I swore he told me he loved me. Maybe he regretted saying it, maybe he was just reacting to me. . . .

February 19, 1996

I'm still not in love . . . like it's expected or something. I'm happy with Jonathan. I'm under no pressure, he respects me and my feelings. In the 3½ months we've been together we haven't fought once. For Valentine's Day I got 2 roses, a box of chocolate-covered cherries, dinner at Ruby Tuesdays, and the opportunity to buy whatever I wanted as long as it'll last. I chose 3 oil candles in the shape of a triangle. Later we went back to his house and watched movies. We never really watch them.

An overwhelming attraction to Tommy [Jonathan's older brother] has captured me. Maybe not overwhelming, but it's there. It was also this time last year Shawn and I were still together. How I pray just to forget him, how I long to fall in love with Jonathan. But I'm not! I don't know how. I won't tell him I love him with feelings for others inside me.

SYLVIA PLATH (1932–1963)
ON FALLING IN LOVE IN
THE SUMMER RAIN

Sylvia Plath was a poet, novelist, and avid diarist. She began her first diary at the age of eleven and continued writing until her tragic suicide at the age of thirty. Sylvia's life was fraught with periods of severe depression, which contributed to the intensity of her work. After graduating from Smith College in 1955, she obtained a Fulbright Scholarship to Cambridge University in London—it was there she met and married British poet Ted Hughes. The downfall of their marriage, provoked by an affair Hughes was having, is said to have been a major catalyst in her ultimate mental demise. In addition to her poetry, Sylvia is also known for her semi-autobiographical novel, *The Bell Jar* (1963). She was the first poet to win a posthumous Pulitzer Prize for her *Collected Poems,* in 1982.

The following entry is one written in July 1950 by the seventeen-year-old Sylvia—the summer before she went to Smith College—as a short-lived romance begins to blossom (read how it ends on page 46). During this period, Sylvia did not date her journal entries but noted what month it was. In this entry, she is every man, woman, and teenager who has ever been made dizzy by the early sensations of love.

July 1950

Emile. There it is; his name. And what can I say? I can say he called for me at nine Saturday night, that I was still weak from having two wisdom teeth out that morning. I can say that we went on a double date dancing at Ten Acres, that I drank five glasses, in the course of the evening, to the bottom, of sparkling tawny ginger ale, while others drank beer. But that's

*not it. Not at all. This is how it was. I dressed slowly, smoothing, per-
fuming, powdering. I sat upstairs in the moist gray twilight, with the
rain trickling down outside, while the family talked and laughed with
company down on the porch. This is I, I thought, the American virgin,
dressed to seduce. I know I'm in for an evening of sexual pleasure. We go
on dates, we play around, and if we're nice girls, we demure at a certain
point. And so it goes. We walked into the bar and sat down, two by two.
E and I had the initial strangeness to rub off. We began to talk—about
the funeral he went to this morning, about his twenty-year-old cousin
who broke his back and is paralyzed for life, about his sister who died of
pneumonia at twelve years. "Good Lord, we're morbid tonight," he
shuddered. And then, "You know something I've always liked . . . I mean
wanted to like? Dark eyes and blonde hair. So we talked about little
things, how words lose their meaning when you repeat them over and
over; how we always liked the age we were at best. . . .*

*There was more small talk, more laughing, sidelong glances, more of
the unspoken physical friction that makes each new conquest so
delightful. In the air was the strong smell of masculinity which creates
the ideal medium for me to exist in. There was something in Emile
tonight, a touch of seriousness, a chemical magnetism, that met my
mood the way pieces of a child's puzzle fit together. He has a fine face,
dark hair, and eyes with enormous black pupils; a straight nose, a
one-sided flashing grin, a clean-cut chin. He is neatly made, with
small, sensitive hands. I knew it would be the way it was. On the dance
floor he held me close to him, the hard line of his penis taut against my
stomach, my breasts aching firm against his chest. And it was like
warm wine flooding through me, a sleepy, electric drowsiness. He
nuzzled his face in my hair, kissed my cheek. "Don't look at me," he
said. "I've just come out of the swimming pool, hot and wet." (God, I
knew it would be like this.) He was looking at me intently, searchingly,
and our eyes met. I went under twice; I was drowning; and he flicked*

his gaze away. On the way to Warrie's at midnight, Emile kissed me in the car, his mouth wet and gentle on mine. At Warrie's, more ginger ale, more beer, and dancing with the dim light from the porch, Emile's body warm and firm against mine, rocking back and forth to the soft, erotic music. . . .

And so we left. It was pouring rain. In the car he put his arm around me, his head against mine, and we watched the streetlights coming at us, blurred and fluid in the watery dark. As we ran up the walk in the rain, as he came in and had a drink of water, as he kissed me good night, I knew that something in me wanted him, for what I'm not sure: He drinks, he smokes, he's Catholic, he runs around with one girl after another, and yet . . . I wanted him. "I don't have to tell you it's been nice," I said at the door. "It's been marvelous," he smiled. "I'll call you. Take care." And he was gone. So the rain comes down hard outside my room, and like Eddie Cohen, I say, ". . . fifteen thousand years—of what? We're still nothing but animals." Somewhere, in his room, Emile lies, about to sleep. God knows what he's thinking.

CHAPTER 3

✳ ✳ ✳

HEARTS THAT HURT

It's hard to fight an enemy who has outposts in your head.

—Sally Kempton

There is nothing—neither hell, nor high water, nor tropical storm, nor meteor shower—that will send you to the stone-cold floor, begging for the mercy of the heavens, like a broken heart. It will seem as though Armageddon has been arranged just for you as all four biblical plagues take place simultaneously in your stomach. Nothing aches more and heartens less. On the upside, there is nothing (nothing!) that will motivate, strengthen, and inspire you to get up and do something with yourself quite like a heart that hurts.

I was watching a documentary on LeAnn Rimes a few years ago (*Behind the Music, E! True Hollywood Story,* or maybe something on CMT; I can't remember), and she spoke of her early singing days, which for her were when she was a child. She overheard her father say something along the lines of "Yeah, she has a good singing voice. But wait until she gets her heart broken, then she'll *really* be able to sing." According to another music legend, No Doubt had achieved some local southern California fame, but it wasn't until bassist Tony Kanal broke up with lead singer Gwen Stefani, after seven years together, that Gwen's song-writing skills were truly polished to perfection.

A scene of broken-heart-inspired creativity rings true in the movie *Something's Gotta Give* (2003). Renowned playwright Erica Barry (Diane Keaton) can't seem to get her writing juices flowing in the way of a new play. She begins to date Harry Sanborn (Jack Nicholson), an overage playboy who is an unlikely candidate for her. To her great surprise, Erica falls in love quickly, then, equally surprisingly and quickly, Harry breaks her heart in the middle of a Manhattan street. She returns, defeated, to her house in the Hamptons and begins to write. She types while her tears fall freely on the keyboard. She cries out loud. She cries first thing in the morning. She cries in the shower. She types. She cries. She laughs at something she has just written, which makes her start crying again. After the montage, she has a finished play that is the "best thing you've ever written," according to her new boyfriend, Julian Mercer (Keanu Reeves).

I'm afraid it's true. If hearts didn't get broken, then poems wouldn't be professed, songs wouldn't be sung, books wouldn't be written, and movies wouldn't be made. Or perhaps they would—love has been known to instigate such acts of expression—but they would be significantly fewer and not nearly as good. The reason being that when you're first falling in love, you're experiencing one set of emotions (happiness, amusement, infatuation), and when you're heart is broken, you're face-to-face with all of your emotions—the strong memory and warmth of yesterday's love followed by confusion, anger, hurt, and sometimes betrayal. Not to mention you're now alone. For a certain period of time, you considered yourself in accordance with another person. Now the beneficiary of your love is out of the equation, and you're left alone with the one person you'd really rather not deal with—yourself. And you have to get to know yourself all over again without your beloved as a distraction. At this low point, creativity, excessive exercise, and ice cream become tantamount to survival.

My journal loves when my heart is broken, because she gets my undivided attention. I, naturally, hate when my main power source isn't functioning properly; however, the act of figuring out how to get the damn thing up and running again has done me more good than harm. It's an operation I'll go so far as to say I'm grateful I taught myself how to perform. I know people who try to avoid broken hearts at all costs. They'll stay in a relationship past its due date so as not to have to deal with actually dumping sour milk down the drain, or they'll quickly fasten themselves to another person and skip any downtime with themselves. I advise against this. I say cut your bungee cord and drop. Once you're at the bottom of the ravine, then you don't have to fear the bottom of the ravine anymore. You won't like it down there. It's dark and cold, but I promise there aren't any monsters. It might take a while, but you'll come up with a clever way to climb out. While you're down there, you'll get to know yourself, and the better you know yourself, the more of an asset you are to everyone else.

In the heartrending Madonna song "Till Death Do Us Part," about the singer's devastating divorce from actor Sean Penn, one of the reasons she cites for the relationship collapse is "You're not in love with someone else. You don't even love yourself." A few albums later, the diva confesses in the song "Secret," "Until I learned to love myself, I was never ever lovin' anybody else." The way Madonna and I figure it, you're always going to have to deal with you whether you're in a relationship or not, so some get-to-know-me time can never be bad. It can be lonely at first, yes, but that, too, shall pass. And if by misfortune's hand you fall into the ravine again, you'll already know your way out.

I'm going to do something a little different here than in the first two chapters, and that is instead of offering an assortment of different broken-heart journal entries of all ages, I'm going to focus on one. This was a big break for me—one of those events in life that you can define by the days before and the days after. The man I write about, Tyler, has already appeared in chapters 1 and 2, and he'll have cameos in chapters 6, 7, and 10. Yeah, he really moved into my mind for an extended period of time. The most embarrassing part is that we didn't date for long at all—a little over two months. (In the movie *Something's Gotta Give*, Harry and Erica were only together for a week, and that makes me feel slightly less crazy. And, yes, I know it's a movie.) It was an experience unlike any other in that I had never before had both the physical and cerebral connection snap so perfectly into place and then have it reciprocated with such enthusiasm. Every sweet advance I made toward him was returned to me tenfold. He always called when he said he would, and sometimes he'd call without warning just to say he was thinking of me. He'd have a rose waiting for me on the dashboard when I got in the car. He introduced me to his friends and invited me to his office Christmas party. When I'd catch him staring in my direction, he'd say, "You have to stop waving your magic wand at me." Oh my, that's corny now. It wasn't then. At the time, I had never heard a set of words so sweet.

Anyway, it ended abruptly. He backed away and then disappeared altogether. I prompted him for an explanation and he said he was getting back together with his ex-girlfriend. That was that. Sort of. When I initially felt my feelings spiraling out of control, I told my journal I wanted to document the experience (page 38)—write a chronicle of falling in love, if you will. The thing is, love does her own thing, and even though Tyler was out of the picture, love wasn't. And so I did fall in love—he just wasn't around to share it with me—and my journal got her chronicle, albeit a little crooked, after all.

A few months after it was over, I got back in touch with him. He told me he was no longer with his girlfriend (not actually true, as I later found out) and we got together. As the date ended, I gave him a letter. It was my final attempt to profess my abiding love and make the case for us to be together. He never responded to it. I moped around for weeks. In addition to not being able to be with him, I was feeling extra sorry for myself because he didn't even acknowledge that he received my letter. I thought it was a very nice letter. I let my roommate read it. She thought it was a very nice letter, too—so nice, in fact, that she asked me to help her write a letter for a guy she was dating. Somewhere between chronically feeling sorry for myself and helping my roommate, Erica, write a letter, I decided to launch a Web site—*letterlover.net*—and offer my letter-writing services to the masses. Just because Tyler didn't like my letter-writing skills didn't mean others wouldn't—humph! Roughly eight months after the site was launched, I was approached by a publisher asking if I'd like to put together a book on letter writing. Five months after that, I had a signed contract and was writing my first book: *For the Love of Letters: A 21st-Century Guide to the Art of Letter Writing*. I'm still a far cry from being LeAnn Rimes or Gwen Stefani, but this is my own private poetic justice, as I can trace the triumph all the way back to him.

As I started writing the book in June 2006, I got in touch with Tyler because there was a letter he had written me way-back-when that I wanted to include, and I needed his legal consent. He responded earnestly, congratulated me, and said I was more than welcome to use his letter. The end of his e-mail included a postscript: "P.S. You must post the letter that you wrote to me a while back. It was the nicest, sexiest, sweetest, and most erotic letter someone has ever given me. I still have it. I don't think I could ever throw it away. So if you don't remember, I will have to forward it to you." *If* I don't remember! A lobotomy couldn't make me forget that letter. Would it have *killed* him to express something along those lines at the time? I relished in his past-due sentiment all the same. As you'll read in subsequent chapters, he and I stayed in touch after that and we got ourselves into one final round of trouble before officially deciding not to stay in touch anymore. No matter what, he's someone I'll always want good things to happen to. How could I not? The man taught me how to sing.

AT TWENTY-FOUR

December 7, 2003

I still haven't heard from Tyler. Of course I wonder what's going on but I am confident that he's a good, no wonderful person and his absence will be justified. And if in the saddening circumstance he has decided we're over then I know he'll be respectful enough to explain things to me. And I'll be upset, but knowing that I had a chance to be with him is enough to make me forever grateful. The chance to be held and to hold such an extraordinary man was amazing. And I'd only want to be with him if I knew for sure I could make him as happy as he makes me—otherwise we'd be incomplete. This makes me realize that I must be on my way to loving him—his happiness means more than mine.

December 14, 2003

I'm coming to the conclusion that love is a place—it is the only place where you lose—completely lose—and completely find yourself on the same spot.

It's an every other minute thing with me. Some moments I know myself well enough to know that he's perfect for me and I lose that seconds later and I don't know what's going on. I'm worried—he's called—but much less frequently. It's too soon for him to be getting comfortable I think. Maybe not—maybe I should be flattered by his comfort. But maybe it's not comfort—maybe it's disinterest. How am I to know? If I ask then I'll scare him away. I keep trying to remind myself that love is patient . . . love is patient . . . love is patient . . . patient-patient-patient. Maybe my love is faster than his. Maybe it's on its way and my patience is required to wait for his. I'm willing to wait—I just want to know if the wait will produce him—will produce us. But I guess that's the risk—waiting and he won't be there. Terrifying. But, yes, he is worth the risk.

*Tell your heart that the fear of suffering is worse
than the suffering itself.*

—Paulo Coelho, one of the many quotes copied in
  my journal from *The Alchemist* in July 2003

December 17, 2003
My chronicle of love has come to a halt. My love subject/focus has
focused on someone else. I ate nothing yesterday. Nothing! My stomach started to digest itself because I hadn't heard from Tyler. When I
got home I was aching and I needed to call him. But for some reason
I held off and checked my e-mail. My heart rested and relaxed when I
saw his name on my computer screen. I knew he'd write me and
everything would be okay. Then my chest caved in and my eyes swelled
when I read the e-mail. He admitted to having strayed away because
"something/an old someone" came back into his life. Devastated. I
think that's the only word there is. Tyler, I had a feeling you were too
good to be true.

But that information is better than no information. It's better to
know this than to know nothing. I couldn't handle it when I thought
he was blowing me off. And if I had to lose him I'd rather lose him to
an "old someone" than a "new someone." Of course he has unsettled
feelings for someone else. We all do. It's just that someone doesn't
always walk back in. But that someone walked back into his life.

I called him as soon as I got his e-mail. I called work. I called his cell.
Sleep didn't happen. Then today I freaked out knowing there'd never be
any closure. I e-mailed him and told him I respect his decision to be with
her and asked that he respect the fact that I can't turn off my feelings
for him, and that he call so we can end on a good note and perhaps talk
again someday. Soon after I sent it, he called. He was busy at work and

wanted to arrange a time when we could talk—we arranged tonight.
I'm fading—based on no sleep and no food—as I wait to hear from him.
He might not call . . . he called . . .

December 18, 2003

Okay, not what I was expected. I was ready to end things and not talk for
a while—hoping to rekindle friendship in the future. But he just expressed how torn he is between me and this other girl. We came to no
conclusions. He did suggest seeing each other this weekend—that could
be very very good or horrid. I'm scared. If it's horrid then I would rather
have ended it last night. Well, at least I can eat now. Lord, give me
strength. Lord, give Tyler strength. May he be with the girl that's best for
him, and please prepare me to deal with the reality that I may not be her.

FYI: We didn't end up getting together. He said he'd call on Saturday
to make plans and never did. It's a cliché in motion.

January 20, 2004

This is a letter I wrote in my journal and never sent nor planned to
send to Tyler. More on unsent letters in a moment.

Dear Tyler,

   I hope you've been well. My year has gotten off to an interesting
start. I have a part-time job at a magazine called *All Woman,* which
should allow me some time to work on my book.* I hope to have most
of it done by this time next year, but who knows how the wheels will
turn.

   I went on a date last night. His name is Stan—he's an accomplished

---

*This was a novel I was working on at the time—more about it in chapter 6.

Shakespearean. He appeared in an independent film called *Sweet Nothings** and is now having his own film produced in Sweden. He speaks several languages and is quite charming. He does have one major flaw—he's not you. I realized this as I was lying on his chest and he had no nipple ring to bite. He and I don't have the same chemistry that you and I do. He's very nice and thoughtful, but my god, Tyler, you're perfect for me. I'm sure the way I feel about Stan is probably the way you feel about me. And now all your carnal energy is focused on her. My great fear is that you hate me. That you're disgusted when you think of me. I pray that's not the case, Tyler, and I pray for you every day. It took a night with another man to make me realize how much I love you.

I love you.

I'm sorry.

I hope you're well.

Samara

EXPRESS YOURSELF IN AN UNSENT LETTER

What you just read is one of the many unsent letters I sent to Tyler. Unsent letters are one of the more popular journal-writing techniques, as they allow for closure and expression that might not come otherwise. It is the practice of writing to someone and saying everything you'd never be able to say, or aren't brave enough to say, in an actual letter. This method really helped me work through my feelings. Because I was writing to Tyler, rather than about him, my thought process was completely different, but knowing that I was never going to send the letter allowed me to open up in ways I never would have otherwise.

*Not the movie's actual title.

One of the most difficult things about a breakup is that the conversation has to stop. You, of course, have ongoing dialogue and inside jokes with another person and, even after the breakup, you naturally motion to call or write them when you have news to share and suffer the sadness when you realize you can't. An unsent letter is a perfect place to put those tiny details you still long to share with the other person.

- **The Unsent Letter You Might Send:** If there is unfinished business between you and another person, it's fair to want to be up front with them. If you are writing a letter under the influence of anger or hurt, though, it's best not to send it right away. Wait a few days or sleep on it, at least. I did this recently. I was furious with a friend of mine, and I wrote her a letter. It was mean and spiteful. I was well aware of how much it would hurt, and I wanted it to hurt. I waited two days, reread it, and ended up saving it to some random file on my desktop. Most of my unsent letters go through a practice round in my journal, but since I had every intention of sending that one, I didn't bother. What stopped me was the fact that I was seething. I knew it was dangerous to send something when I could be considered temporarily insane. I haven't always been this discerning when so emotional, but it's the same rule that applies when you drunk-dial too many times—you learn to stop yourself. Writing something out, then waiting to send it, enables you to unload the excess anger and ideally have a more open and productive exchange with the person when you're ready, and it can stop you from burning bridges.

- **The Unsent Letter You'll Never Send:** Knowing you'll never send a letter gives you license to say anything. You can be rude, irreverent, and brutally honest. Tell them what you really think. Saying all that you feel and not being interrupted is great and necessary to experience on occasion. Oftentimes, it's difficult to be completely candid, even in your journal. But as soon as you trick yourself into thinking you're not writing in a journal, you're writing a letter to someone who pushes all your buttons, then you'll lift the straight-forward floodgates.

THE BLIND DATE THAT BROKE THE CAMEL'S BACK

Before I dated Tyler, I had been single for about a year and a half, but I didn't really notice. I was a free spirit—dating every now and again, but not looking for anything permanent. After Tyler, I felt like the Lone Ranger. I was aware, at all times, of my single, solitary existence. It was then I entered the conundrum many of us find ourselves in: You meet people who want to date you and people you want to date, but you can't for the life of you find someone who plays both roles. I lived there for a while—bouncing back and forth between hoping something would work out and not wanting it to with certain men. I suppose I technically still live there now, except my outlook is drastically different from what it once was.

What forever changed my perspective on being single was a blind date. Chloé, a good friend, called me one afternoon and said, "Oh my God! I met your husband." She proceeded to tell me about Evan—a friend of her boyfriend Tony—who she had met the night before. She told me he was big into doing outdoorsy things and also a magnetic conversationalist. Tall. Cute. Those qualifications sounded good to me, but I was especially intrigued because in the four years I had known Chloé, she had never tried to set me up with anyone. She's not a careless matchmaker—much thought goes into her arrangements.

I met Evan by way of a double blind date. I was anxious for all the typical reasons: What if I wasn't attracted to him or what if I was and he wasn't drawn to me? The one thing I knew for sure was that we'd be able to talk. Even if we weren't feeling each other romantically, I would still enjoy a get-to-know-you conversation. Chloé's initial screening sold me on that. Watching me fidget nervously, my friend leaned into me and thoughtfully reassured, "You look very pretty." When Evan arrived, I was taken with him instantly. He, well, I'll let my twenty-six-year-old self tell the story:

April 23, 2006

My heart continues its search to no avail. Chloé and Tony introduced me to a seemingly great guy last night. Evan—attractive (curly hair), insightful, at ease with himself. The four of us had a great (I've used that word twice unfortunately) time until about 1/1:30 the two of them decided to go. Evan invited me to continue on and I was glad he did. Our conversation dipped below the surface several times, and I enjoyed all sides of him. When we moved from bar to bar he held on to me tightly beneath my umbrella. He touched my waist freely in an inoffensive and warm way. By the time 4 a.m. came I was very excited about the prospect of seeing him again soon. As we left the last bar he asked me if I wanted to go home with him. I said no with a smile. He asked if I was sure. I was surprised he asked again but responded in an equally friendly manner, "Yes, I'm sure. Next time. Some other time. Just not tonight." He continued to ask, and I continued to say no. Finally he said, "At least let me get you a cab." He hailed one and then asked if I wanted us to go to my place instead. At this point my heart had no choice but to start sinking. I thought we had a good time and he might want to see me again. His intentions were well laid out at this point. He opened the cab door and didn't ask for my number, so I mumbled something about us seeing each other again. He pulled out his business card and handed it to me. I think that upset me the most. So I handed my business card right back to him. Before he closed the cab door he sat down and said (one more time), "I still think you should let me go home with you."

"Good night, Evan," I said.

Once I found myself interested in Evan and fully engaged in our conversation, I still left ample room for him not to reciprocate—that's usually the way of it. I waited for him to take his exit when Chloé and Tony left, as that would have been the easy, cordial route. When he didn't do that, I thought maybe we were actually sharing an attraction, but I still left room for him to shake my hand at the end of the evening and say, "It was nice meeting you." I hadn't left any room for him to treat me as if I had been hired. I'm sure part of the reason he kept asking me to go home with him was that I was saying no in an amicable way (amicable yet still clear and consistent), but I was genuinely confused. He hadn't even tried to kiss me, which I foolishly thought meant he was waiting until our first official date, and there he was asking in no uncertain terms if he could bend me over his bedside.

I can laugh loudly at the situation now (and Chloé and I entertainingly retell it all the time), but at the time, I was devastated. Chloé called me first thing Sunday morning to find out what happened. "Tony and I are dying to know!" I, still a little shaken and unsure, just told her we had a nice time, but he didn't ask for my number and I doubted I'd hear from him. It wasn't until a few nights later, when she and I were out to dinner, that I told her how many times (an estimated twelve) he asked me to go home with him. She slowly put her hand to her mouth and said, "I am so sorry. I'm sick to my stomach right now."

In the days that followed, my emotional tectonic plates shifted. I can tell how severe the transformation was based on the unresponsive way I wrote in my journal the morning after. I was clearly upset but not as distressed as I was to become. During that period, I wasn't dealing with Evan as much as I was dealing with Evan on top of everybody else. When one situation doesn't work out, it conjures up harsh images of all the others that didn't work out either. It reminds you that you're single and you might just have to stay that way. It was that notion I forced myself to face. I looked it right in the eye until it broke me. Every time it upset me, I'd say it again until I was more upset. Until eventually I arrived at the point where I couldn't be upset about it anymore. I let the reality marinate within me. I then decided my days might actually be much easier if I let up and stopped playing "insert man here" and if I approached my life as if it were just going to be me, myself, and I. This isn't to say I wouldn't welcome love with open arms—I am aware of and grateful for my capacity to love. I just decided I wasn't officially looking anymore. If I got married, it would be because the universe put in my path a man who made me want marriage—instead of the idea of marriage making me want to find a man (any man). This was a difficult and liberating conclusion to come to.

You will be pleased to know that the natural longing to share time, space, and physical connection with another human being does not go away. I know. I tried very hard to make that need go away. What I was able to do was alter it from being a constant craving in my life to now being something I only feel when actually faced with a man who I think would really rock my world. What began as self-pity became a surge of empowerment. To me, this decision was the difference between considering myself an incomplete person until a relationship came along to fill the void and considering myself a complete person willing to share her life with another complete person if the opportunity presented itself. And if the opportunity never presents itself, then my life does not go unfulfilled. As a direct result of this situation, I decided that single or married, blonde or brunette (or even sassy redhead), my life would not disappoint anyone—least of all me.

SYLVIA PLATH (1932–1963) ON BREAKING HIS HEART AND YOUR OWN ON A LATE-SUMMER NIGHT

I hope it's not too unorthodox to include a second Sylvia Plath journal entry. Truth be told, I could have ended every chapter with one of Sylvia's entries (it was difficult not to). She's a marvel. Her poems, letters, and journal entries hold me graciously by the throat. She writes brilliant things like "There are times when a feeling of expectancy comes to me, as if something is there, beneath the surface of my understanding, waiting for me to grasp it." Anyway! Things with Emile began in July and then ended in August (seven journal entries later)—just before Sylvia went off to college.

August 1950

Now I'll never see him again, and maybe it's a good thing. He walked out of my life last night for once and for all. I know with sickening certainty that it's the end. There were just two dates we had, and the time he came over with the boys, and tonight. Yet I liked him too much—way too much, and I ripped him out of my heart so it wouldn't get to hurt me more than it did. Oh, he's magnetic, he's charming; you could fall into his eyes. Let's face it: his sex appeal was unbearably strong. I wanted to know him—the thoughts, the ideas behind the handsome, confident, wise-cracking mask. "I've changed," he told me. "You would have liked me three years ago. Now I'm a wiseguy." We sat together for a few hours on the porch, talking, and staring at nothing. Then the friction increased, centered. His nearness was electric in itself. "Can't you see," he said. "I want to kiss you." So he kissed me, hungrily, his eyes shut, his hand warm, curved burning into my stomach. "I wish I hated you," I said. "Why did you come?" "Why? I wanted your company. Alby and Pete were going to the ball game, and I couldn't see that. Warrie and Jerry were going drinking; couldn't see that either." It was past eleven; I walked out the door with him and stepped outside into the cool August night. "Come here," he said. "I'll whisper something: I like you, but not too much. I don't want to like anybody too much." Then it hit me and I just blurted, "I like people too much or not at all. I've got to go down deep, to fall into people, to really know them." He was definite, "Nobody knows me." So that was it; the end. "Goodbye for good, then," I said. He looked hard at me, a smile twisting his mouth, "You lucky kid; you don't know how lucky you are." I was crying quietly, my face contorted. "Stop it!" The words came like knife thrusts, and then his gentleness, "In case I don't see you, have a nice time at Smith." "Have a hell of a nice life," I said. And he walked off down the path with his jaunty, independent stride. And I stood there where he left me, tremulous with love and longing, weeping in the dark. That night it was hard to get to sleep.

CHAPTER 4

✳ ✳ ✳

THE SPIRIT IS WILLING

We are not born all at once, but by bits. The body first, and the sprit later.
Our mothers are racked with the pains of our physical birth; we
ourselves suffer the longer pains of our spiritual growth.

—Mary Antin

(Copied into my journal on August 8, 1998)

I realize much of my journal reads like *Are You There God? It's Me, Samara*. Although unlike the character Margaret in Judy Blume's celebrated novel, I did not grow up with one Christian and one Jewish parent but rather with two devout Christians. Aside from sporadic vacations and the occasional illness, I have gone to church every Sunday of my life. This probably hasn't been too hard to believe up until this point, but it will become more difficult to reconcile as you read on. I am a versatile sinner who's been known to play her St. Augustine card more than once. The fourth-century philosopher and theologian once said, "God, give me chastity and continence—but not just now."

My upbringing was very Christian—if you can qualify it. I grew up in the Episcopal Church, an establishment that lives on the line between

Catholicism and Protestantism; it assigns itself to neither and possesses qualities of both. I sang in the choir, served as an acolyte, and belonged to the youth group. My extended family is Catholic, and so all the weddings, funerals, and services following cousin sleepovers I attended were of that denomination. In high school, I was part of two youth groups not associated with my church—one was Methodist and the other a nondenominational, evangelical organization. By "very Christian," I mean I was exposed to many of the faces of Christianity (and there are many more). I have worshiped in High Church as well as on cold nights around a campfire. I have prayed surrounded by the sounds of hymns and the smell of incense as well as running late between class periods. I see the value in both.

I realize not everyone enjoys prayer, and that many are wary of organized religion or religion in general. I understand this—though I think it has more to do with the defective human beings who "organize" the religion than with the religion itself. I was on a retreat weekend my freshman year of college and met a hippie-looking man with his jet-black hair pulled into a loose ponytail. He and I got to talking, and I asked him what religion he was. He thought for a moment and said, "I don't have a religion. I have a spirituality." I loved that answer. I wanted it on a T-shirt. On her Web site, Judy Blume echoes a similar sentiment by associating herself with her well-known character: "And like Margaret, I had a very personal relationship with God that had little to do with organized religion. God was my friend and confidant." Oddly enough, I identify with this statement, though my background has a great deal to do with organized religion. I like having a relationship with God or a higher power apart from any establishment.

We all come from drastically different religious and spiritual backgrounds. But whatever your personal experience, a journal is a great medium for gaining further understanding into your voyage thus far. Whether it's coming to terms with or laying to rest the religion of your childhood, adopting a belief system for the first time in your life, lashing out at the universe for being so shady and allowing bad things to happen, or officially deciding that there is no God, writing about it can be restorative. If you're interested in exploring your spiritual self further, before you up and go to a worship service of any sort or pack for a holy pilgrimage, write out some of your thoughts and questions on what is or isn't occupying the heavens and what you hope to find as you seek.

Although I have never (or rarely, I shouldn't say never) doubted the sovereignty of God, it's only natural to grow up and question the things you've been told. My journal bears continual witness to the many certainties and uncertainties of my spiritual journey. Sometimes whoever or whatever I was writing about would lead me into prayer, which I often included as part of the entry. Other times, I'd feel spiritually vacant or fully inspired. Whatever my spiritual status, my journal is ready to receive it, and this enables me the chance to look over my doubts and continue thinking them through or relish and relive powerful and uplifting moments.

In my twenties, I have had the pleasure of discovering that I have been in the right religious place all along. I find the Episcopal Church welcomes the inquiries of its members. There is an open dialogue kept between clergy and congregation, and seldom is anyone told that they are flat-out wrong and not allowed to believe something. The views of this progressive institution surely shaped and ultimately matched my own. In addition to the prayers I've written regarding specific situations that appear throughout this book, here are a few of my spiritual struggles and triumphs:

AT EIGHTEEN

December 12, 1997

It is a day, a real day, a genuine day. To whom do I owe this day? Why is it that I now officially possess the ability to disregard my creator? Every night for the majority of my life I ended my day with a prayer, but that happens no more. I long to pray, but I don't know how to address my Lord. Isn't that nonsense!! He's always willing to be addressed. Do I apologize? Do I beg forgiveness? What do I do?

AT NINETEEN

October 22, 1998

I often wonder why daydreams, day illusions, and even day fantasies are allowed. Why would God allow me to imagine a moral victory or a positive healing of emotional wounds and not allow me to achieve it? I suppose it's deeply rooted in my nature to expect too much. But I have been aptly blessed and forever cursed by my ability to daydream. Wherever daily paths lead me I am always able to fall away into my fantasies, sometimes demure and other times less than decorous.

AT TWENTY-THREE

June 28, 2003

The spirit is willing but the flesh is weak. The flesh is weak. The flesh is weak. The flesh is remarkably weak. The flesh is curiously weak. The flesh is shamefully weak.

Lord, please put forgivness in my forecast.

AT TWENTY-FOUR

February 2004

A few weeks ago Peter said this in church: "When you get to Heaven God won't ask to see your trophies, he'll ask to see your scars."

AT TWENTY-SIX

January 21, 2006

I'm at the Holy Cross Monastery in West Park, NY. It's a glorious hour and a half away from Manhattan up the Hudson. I'm here with the Grace Church 20s/30s group. We settled in nicely. I've written the monastic schedule on the previous page. We have five services a day, but honestly I could have more. There's such comfort in the liturgy and such meaning in the motions of the monks. There are a few things taking place in the city right now that could worry me, but there is no worry within.

EXPRESS YOURSELF WITH QUESTIONS AND CONCERNS

We all have a gut reaction to God. *Yes!* or *No!* or *No, except when I'm on an airplane and there's turbulence!* Writing out queries and reservations is a good way to locate the source of your notion of God. In high school, I had a friend who was an outspoken atheist. I asked her why she didn't believe in God and she said, "Because priests rape little boys." Tragically, that's true, and I didn't attempt a rebuttal because I believe in

God despite knowing well that horrific things like that happen and because trying to convince her to do the same would have been futile. But it made me wonder how much of her not believing in God was not believing in human beings.

In elementary school, I was the only one of my friends who wasn't Catholic, and they liked to make sure I felt left out on account of this fact (ladies, you could have been a little more creative). They would talk about what happened at CCD (Confraternity of Christian Doctrine religious instruction) the night before and mock that it was a pity I wasn't there. The Catholic Church left a bad taste in my mouth for a long time, and it took me a while to figure out that this was the actual source—well, that and the fact that I was never allowed to take Communion. Now I have a whole new set of adult issues with the Catholic Church (wink).

The point is, so many of our ideas about what religion is and isn't come from other people, and it's worth ripping apart these notions to find what our beliefs actually are. Even people such as myself, who choose to stay with the religion or belief system they were raised in, need to step outside of it and double-check that they do, in fact, believe and aren't just going through the motions. It's unwise to robotically believe what someone has handed you on a scroll, because then your beliefs are not your own. Blind faith and even blind lack of faith don't serve much purpose. The way to obtain a spirituality rather than a religion is to come to your own conclusions and have them with you at all times, not just during services. And, of course, at the bottom of someone's belief barrel, it may be that there is no God. I would much rather have afternoon tea with an atheist who has put a great deal of thought into his or her stance than with someone who shrugs ambiguous shoulders and says, "I dunno." Some ways to consider your spiritual status:

- **Locate the Source:** Write about your earliest experiences with or without religion—you went to worship and none of your friends did, or all of your friends went to worship and you didn't. Did you feel left out? Did you grow up surrounded by people who believed what you did and weren't exposed to any other belief systems? What, if anything, have you wondered but were afraid to ask? Write a spiritual autobiography, and you may uncover, as I uncovered with my Catholic friends, the source of some of your anxieties, objections, and hostilities.

- **Get Angry:** Life is completely unfair and hard to navigate through. What kind of loving creator would throw us into such a mess? There's plenty in life to be pissed off about. There are many things religious institutions do to infuriate the masses. It's more than acceptable to be angry about such things and to present these frustrations to the powers that be. (Think Lieutenant Dan in the movie *Forrest Gump* as he declares a showdown between himself and God while fastened to the top of a boat during a hurricane.)

- **Write Prayers and Meditations:** If you do believe in "God" or a higher power and pray in silence or aloud, then consider writing your prayers. It is an easy way to expand on whatever is plaguing your mind or to solidify a moment of appreciation and is a powerful way to close a journal entry. If you don't necessarily call God, God, but do spend quiet time meditating, consider writing the things you meditate on and the insights you have during this time.

ON THE UNIVERSE

Throughout this book, I often refer to "the universe," and I wanted to clarify that I am using it in a spiritual context, synonymous with God. This was one of the first spiritual declarations I made for myself by myself with the help of the book *The Alchemist*. This well-known tome manages to be highly insightful and spiritual without tying itself to any particular religion. The book references the universe itself as a higher power. I have copied many lines into my journal, including this one on July 19, 2003: "When you really want something, the universe always conspires in your favor."

I believe the universe is the system of coincidence, or rather, the system of noncoincidence. My mother often says, "There are no coincidences, only God-instances," and while I think that that execution is a little cheesy, I grasp the concept. And that's how I see the universe—as a system put in place by God. This system has us, by all appearances, interacting in a completely random way, when, I believe, it's actually quite organized. The universe is what guides me to call my friend Zazel, and, after more than six weeks of not being in touch, she answers the phone and says, "I was just starting to write you an e-mail." It's what stops you from getting one job because a better opportunity is on its way. It's what instigates the death of a relationship for the birth of creativity. It's why the world is so small. Anyway, that's what I mean when I refer to the universe, and all other interpretations of the universe are welcome.

JOYCE CAROL OATES (B. 1938) ON CONTEMPLATING YOUR PLACE IN THE UNIVERSE

Joyce Carol Oates is the author of over thirty novels—the first published in 1964 at the age of twenty-six—and there are two forthcoming. She has also written many short story collections, several plays, and volumes of poetry, as well as essays and literary criticism. Her novel *Them* won the National Book Award in 1970. *Prolific* isn't even the right word to describe her, and she is the only journal-writing legend featured in this book who is still living. When she began journaling at the age of thirty-four, she didn't plan on it playing an extended role in her life. In the foreword to *The Journal of Joyce Carol Oates (1973–1982)*, she says she saw her journal as something "that would not last beyond the strain of the sabbatical year, or beyond the mood of loneliness, dislocation, and general melancholy-malaise that seemed to have descended upon me at the time." The journal lasted much longer than anticipated and is now a keyhole for devotees to peek into and see the mind of this inexhaustible talent at work. Joyce admits that she's not one who likes to reread her journals and old letters, saying "revisiting the past is like biting into a sandwich in which you've been assured there are only a few, really very few, bits of ground glass." In the following entry, Joyce contemplates incorporating a mystical experience into a novel she is working on, and this leads her down the path of considering the concept of the universe and her place in it.

February 17, 1973

The memory of that odd, inexplicable experience at our Dunraven flat. Must dramatize it somehow in a story, a novel . . . Corinne of Lucien Florey. *But I despair getting it right.*

Perhaps I'm too close to the experience; I'm too attached.

Can one really believe in the playfulness of the universe?—and its beauty?

In theory, yes. Very readily.

In experience . . . ?

No, such beliefs, however passionately held, are a mockery of our ordinary perceptions. "God is love," etc. An insult to those who suffer. "God is God is all": The sum total of the universe. Neither good nor evil. Just an immense democracy. One alternates between embracing such a conviction . . . and running from it in horror.

The hubris of "accepting" the universe.

What am I, finally, but a field of experience . . . a network of events . . . ? They are held in suspension, in a sense, so long as "I" exist. When "I" am dissolved they too are dissolved (except of course for those things that have been recorded in print). Even so . . .

CHAPTER 5

SENSE OF SELF

Self-love is not so vile a sin as self-neglecting.

—William Shakespeare

(This quote is embedded in a stained-glass window at the University of
Pennsylvania's Fisher Fine Arts Library, where I wrote this chapter.)

In order to write a nonfiction book, you have to present the publisher
with a proposal—an outline of what you plan to do, what topics you
plan to address, and the order you plan to address them in. During the
writing process, both parties—author and publisher—leave some room
to stray from the proposal, as creativity inevitably takes on a life of its
own. The final product must, however, bear some resemblance to the
original layout. I have managed to match my manuscript with my proposal thus far. This chapter, however, is a deviation. I didn't plan to write
it—it asked politely to be written.

While rereading my journals, I continually encountered entries that
appeared to me as the emotional equivalent of math work—the kind you
have to show on algebra and trigonometry tests. The answer doesn't count
unless the work is shown. In these entries, I am quite literally working

myself out. Figuring out how I feel about me, the idea of me, about how I look, about what I do, about what I don't do, and about me in relation to others. Oddly enough, knowing yourself isn't a given, and sometimes we have to do extracurricular work to figure out exactly who we are.

When I was in college, I came up with the notion of and really wanted to find an "honest mirror." That is a mirror that tells me what other people see when they look at me. I will never have the pleasure and the pain of looking in such a mirror because everyone approaches me with vastly different sets of experience behind their eyes. Someone who was mocked in grade school by a very tall bully might subconsciously (or consciously) hold my height against me. A fellow tall girl will take refuge in exchanging glances with me, and I with her. We share an understanding. In high school, I hated my tallness and would wince when looking at the girls who could look me in the eye—not wanting to give them a chance to be attractive because I loathed our shared quality. We look at others, and feel them looking back, with our own set of preconceived notions, preferences, and insecurities in mind.

Having an acute sense of self is about balance. You have to be kind to yourself, but not so lenient that you can't be occasionally critical and enact self-discipline—and not so critical that you spend too much time degrading yourself. You have to be confident in your abilities and talents, but not so much that watching someone else win makes you furious and negates what you know yourself to be capable of. You have to care about other people without letting what they think affect you too much. That last one is tough. Too often, we get our sense of self from other people and grant them far too much power over how we feel. However, we still have to interact with each other and therefore it's impossible, and unwise, not to care about others at all.

I'm not saying any of the above is easy, nor am I saying I've got it all down. I am saying a healthy sense of self is a difficult and worthy goal. Knowing your physical and emotional strengths and weaknesses and

being able to accept them is key to the well-lived life. People with no or a
very low sense of self or a haughty sense of self can be hard not only on
themselves but also on the rest of us. In a basic way, someone who has no
idea that they talk too loudly or complain too often is the one avoided at
a party. The girl who always puts herself down in a social setting with the
thinly veiled hope that everyone else will lift her back up can be the dark
cloud over happy hour, as can the girl who is so preoccupied with talking
about how great she is that she doesn't take a minute to (1) breathe or (2)
ask how you are. It all goes back to balance—confidence and humility
working constantly to keep each other in check.

   This, more than anything, is what a journal lends to—finding your
sense of self. If you're working on your public-speaking skills, experts
often recommend you videotape yourself, so you can see what you're doing wrong. I tend to find this practice awkward—I'll forever hate the
sound of my voice—and ultimately very helpful. When watching the
tape, I see the difference between what I thought I was doing and what I
was actually doing. Journaling about yourself can offer the same outsider
perspective. You may think you're living one way, but your writing says
otherwise. Some of my math teachers were kind enough to give points for
the work even if the answer ended up being wrong, so I say that's how we
go about doing this, too. Write out the work in the equation of yourself,
and don't worry about the definitive answer just yet. It's a lifelong process, and herein lies the benefit of aging—knowing yourself all the more.
Here are some of my self-savvy insights so far:

AT EIGHTEEN

September 20, 1997
Let me be logical here. No, let me be crazy. I've never felt comfortable in
the presence of logic. It's always mocked me, there is always one right

answer . . . just one right answer . . . only one. You can't penetrate logic and turn it into many things for it's only one thing. No exploration, no deeper meaning, just one answer to one question and no more.

November 1997

I enjoy watching my lips move. My lips are incredibly fleshy so my mouth requires more effort than most mouths. I enjoy looking at my face. Because it's beautiful. But it's only beautiful when I'm alone. As soon as another enters my presence the beauty fades. Why must it be that way? Why can't they see me when I'm pretty? Why can't my face even be appropriate for them? What do they want? It's so unhealthy for me to be here like this admiring myself. Because my position will be shattered as soon as I walk out the door. I'm the only one who'll ever be obsessed with me. The angel of doubt has entered, but we'll push him away . . . we must!

January 6, 1998

← Same day.

I swear this is just a part of my story... right? My apathy, my compulsive daydreams, my sloth, my vanity, my fading sense of direction. I am not proud of any of these, I am not proud of myself. I have accomplished nothing! If death captures me tomorrow then that's it! It's over. No one will remember me. I'll have done nothing that is worthy of recognition and the trouble is I don't know where to begin. I think I'll go get my eyebrows waxed.

AT NINETEEN

April 5, 1999

I had a revelation. My choice in men . . . they've all been a bit cocky and too self-confident. I wanted to be a part of their self-assured ways. I wanted them to distinguish me. They'll never distinguish me, so I'll have to distinguish myself.

I want by understanding myself, to understand others.
I want to be all that I am capable of being.

—Katherine Mansfield, copied in my journal May 18, 2000

AT TWENTY-SEVEN

April 2, 2007

It's in these moments—these tender, vulnerable moments—the writer in me comes out. She moves. She shivers. I tell her to go away. I say, "I am comfortable now. I don't need you anymore." She says nothing. She just keeps tossing and turning until I can't take anymore. I have to set her free.

EXPRESS YOURSELF IN A STREAM OF CONSCIOUSNESS

Stream-of-consciousness writing is mental anarchy and spring-cleaning all in one. It's like going into the basement, turning the tables over, breaking the records in half, cutting the stuffed animals open with a sharp pair of scissors (and feeling much better afterward), then putting it all out just in time for the garbage man to collect. In the book *Journal to the Self: Twenty-two Paths to Personal Growth*, author Kathleen Adams, M.A., notes that the purpose of the stream-of-consciousness technique is, "to invite the subconscious and the unconscious minds to empty their purses on the table before you so that you may sift through and see what has been forgotten, what has been overlooked, what can be discarded." Stream-of-consciousness writing is cathartic. Ignore everything you ever learned about writing and just write. Here's an example straight from the back of my brain:

> I fee it when competition comes in first. Empty. Emotive. Dare
> I say yes? The dark is daunting. Life looks like a dirty razor with
> sunshine on the other side. I think you think you've won. I
> wrap the finish line neatly around myself.

That's all there is to it. Your uninterrupted thoughts glide freely across the page in random order. It doesn't always happen right away (don't get frustrated if it doesn't), but it will grant you insight into some of the things plaguing you. What appears to be something your significant other is doing wrong is actually your lack of patience. What appears to be lethargy at work is really fear of your ideas being rejected. If you write and find yourself saying, "Wow. Did I really just write that?" then good. You've struck a chord within yourself. You won't like everything you read, but that's okay. You have to walk into the basement, turn the lights on, and look at the mess before you can clean it up.

- **Choose a Word:** The great thing about stream-of-consciousness writing is, there's no pressure. The stress of wanting to eloquently recount the musical you saw the other night is not there. You can start by writing about anything and stop when you feel you're done. If you're having trouble getting started, pick a word. Any word. Every word will lead you someplace; it'll remind you of something. *Apple* could remind you of your mother's pie, Gwyneth Paltrow's daughter, or the orchards where you and your friends used to smoke pot. *Spray paint* could make you dizzy (think sniffing) at the idea alone or remind you that you always wanted to be a graffiti artist. A word that you don't know the definition of can inspire you to make one up—then your mind is off and running.

- **Choose an Emotion:** If there's an emotion you've been overwhelmed with recently or a situation you keep replaying in your head that conjures a certain feeling, you might want to start there. Ramble on about this feeling and tell of your earliest memories encountering it. Also consider beginning with an emotion you haven't felt in a while. You can ask Love and Bliss where they've been lately. Or you can tell Gluttony you're glad she's gone for good.

- **Pose a Question:** If a single word or emotion doesn't get your consciousness stream flowing, you can try asking yourself a question. Something as simple as "Where do I want to be?" can yield a million different answers. Your interpretation of the question can be very telling. You could say, "In Curtis's arms," "Higher in the ranks at work," or, "In Fiji," and you'll know where your priorities lie. Take it from there and continue explaining why that's ideal for you.

SENSE OF ANOTHER'S SELF

As a parent, as a sibling, and most often as a friend, you're bound to witness someone you're close to, waging a public battle with their sense of self. It's difficult to be a bystander when this happens. You think this person is wonderful and, try as you might, you can't seem to convince them of that. I came across such an instance in one of my college journals. I was nineteen at the time:

March 1999

If I could stamp out anything it would be low self-esteem. Last night at an SAE* mixer** Linda stood beside me and said, "Samara, I need boys to find me attractive." My heart shuddered. What was I to say to her? I had admired her for so long. I'd give anything for her clever wit. Her personality is vibrant and people are attracted to that. She's not Helen of Troy, but she's still cute and she always has the perfect thing to say. So there we were. If I had her personality I'd have a much better chance of captivating the men I want, I'm sure. And she simply wanted a few boys to display their interest in her appearance. I don't know why the grass is greener. I don't know why some women go through life resenting their bodies and hating their faces. I don't know why some women are blessed with beauty but can't seem to find love. If I could make Linda and every other woman walk around with confidence but not conceit then I certainly would.

I hadn't thought about this situation or Linda in years, but rereading the entry brought me right back to the damp basement we were standing

*Sigma Alpha Epsilon fraternity.
**The "Greek" word for party.

in and the tub of jungle juice we were standing next to. I was beside my-self at her confession. She was one of the funnier people I knew, and I was semi-shocked that she was content being friends with me in the first place. I thought my personality was too bland for a live wire like her—maybe she just needed a straight man. This was the first time she opened up to me about her inner demons, and there were a handful of other times to follow. Each time, I told her how hilarious and pretty I thought she was—a killer combo—but she didn't want to hear that just from me. She wanted to hear it from the boys, which was understand-able.

A journal is a place where we write about our own problems. This is more than fine and to be expected. Taking some time to write about other people's problems, however, can give insight not only into human nature as a whole but also into yourself. It is a human habit (flaw, short-coming, deficiency) to dish out advice left and right to other people—telling them how they can fix their lives and relationships—but we don't always care to examine our own situations so thoroughly. I'm one who's always up for telling a girlfriend, "He's bad for you. Leave him," yet it's a frosty day in hell when I can give myself that pill. I'd be quick to tell Linda she shouldn't be so down on herself, but find it much more difficult to offer myself the same counsel in notably low moments. Spread out someone else's issues in your journal sometime, and react to that person's problem just as you would if you were speaking with them. If you're really brave, you'll reread the recommendations you gave them if and when you find yourself in a similar circumstance.

TENNESSEE WILLIAMS (1911–1983) ON PONDERING YOUR PLACE IN THIS STRANGE THING CALLED LIFE

Tennessee Williams, born Thomas Lanier Williams, was reared in Mississippi and Missouri, and went on to become one of the most notorious playwrights of the twentieth century. The second of three children, his upbringing was filled with tension. His parents, a shoe salesman and the daughter of a minister, often engaged in violent arguments that disturbed his older sister, Rose, who was eventually diagnosed with schizophrenia and spent most of her adult life in and out of mental institutions. Cornelius Williams (father) often favored his younger son, Dakin, over Tennessee. Troubled family relationships is an autobiographical theme that permeates Tennessee's plays—notably *Cat on a Hot Tin Roof*, which he won his second Pulitzer Prize for in 1955. His first Pulitzer was for *A Streetcar Named Desire* in 1948. Tennessee began keeping a journal in his mid-twenties and continued until two years before his death at the age of seventy-one. In the following entry, written at the age of twenty-five, he takes some time to reflect on himself amidst his family, friendships, and writing pursuits.

Sunday, 5 July 1936

I'm a swell one to accuse anybody of lacking a sense of humor. Apparently I've completely lost my own. Been brooding and whining to myself continually the last few days. Fancy myself for being sick and refuse to do any work. Of course it is exhaustingly hot and this house—this domestic life—is quite fiendish. The old man like a dormant volcano, mother *nagging a great deal, Rose and Dakin in continual stupid quarrels. Even I cannot keep my temper and act childishly. How stupid we all are! It is impossible to think of such fools as we are having immortal souls—we have plenty to eat but actually squabble over food sometimes as though we were starving. We say petty, annoying things to each other—today I feel as though I dislike them all and could feel no sorrow if they were all gone. Dreadful to hate everyone as I do sometimes. And yet I have such profound capacity for love and even for happiness. I live in some kind of cage—or enchantment—<u>nothing happens</u>—I seem unable to take any <u>action</u>—just drift along haphazardly from day to day—wondering what will turn up—I can't force myself to do anything—I've given up making myself write that verse drama—No use—If I don't want to write I <u>can't</u> write—I've written two short stories lately—one pretty good I now think—"Ten Minute Stop"—sent to <u>Story</u>. My story in <u>Manuscript</u> will be printed this month says Rood. He wrote me a long letter explaining the Fascist peril which I express doubts concerning in my letter to him.*

I've made my peace with Wil Wharton and sent Clark a letter of apology—no answer as yet—Doubt that I will get one—I'm sometimes ashamed of myself for being such a <u>worm</u>.

Dear Grand and Grandfather arrive this evening to be with us while the others are touring. Those are two persons I do love and always shall—more than anybody else in the world. My grandmother's got more God in her than any thing or anybody else I've yet discovered on earth! When I think of God I think of her—

But it is hard to think of God these days except with a feeling of ~~dull~~ sorrowful perplexity.

<u>*How strange this life is!!!!!*</u>

※ ❋ ※

CHAPTER 6

WHILE YOU WERE SLEEPING

A dream is a wish your heart makes
When you're fast asleep

**—Lyric line from a song written and composed by
Mack David, Al Hoffman, and Jerry Livingston for
the Walt Disney film *Cinderella***

There are people who interpret dreams for a living. Some approach the interpretation of dreams in a mystical, New Age–type way, while others prefer the more scientific, psychoanalytical method of examination. I have limited knowledge and can't really comment on either school of thought, other than it seems they are in agreement that working with and understanding dreams can contribute to mental stability and inner awareness. The only thing I know for certain about dreams is that I have them, and I write about them.

I, like many, believe that dreams are the bridge between the conscious and the subconscious. They are a constant reminder that there is always more to explore in our own minds. Personally, I've never felt my dreams were telling me about my future or my past but rather were inviting me, for better or worse, to face my present. I can usually wake up and think, *Oh yeah, that makes sense. It's been on my mind lately.* Oftentimes, I find my dreams tell me that I'm not thinking about something enough, or that I'm thinking about it too much. Naturally, there is plenty of dream material that I can't even begin to interpret, and I have to really sift through it to find meaning. How does one sift thoroughly through one's dreams? You guessed it—by writing them down. Journaling about dreams requires you to think about them longer than you normally would, and you might find yourself going so far as to really read into them. This lends to a greater understanding between the conscious and the subconscious.

If asked before working on this book whether I wrote about dreams a lot, I would have said no. I'd have said I kept a dream journal once in college but it only lasted about ten entries. And I would have been dead wrong. Apparently, I write about dreams all the time. While going through my journals, I consistently found—smashed between the heartaches, prayers, and prom plans—detailed entries about my dreams. I was pleasantly surprised. It felt like I kept finding four-leaf clovers. *Oh, there's another one! And another!* I'm sure these don't stand out in my memory because dreams are a very in-the-moment experience. You remember the dream and are still affected by it maybe the hour, sometimes a few hours, after you wake up, but by the end of the day, it's usually gone up in smoke. In the book *The New Diary,* author Tristine Rainer writes about dreams:

> *Generally, dreams in and of themselves are neither useful nor interesting for very long. It is the interrelationship between your dreams and your life that gives meaning to both. And it is this interrelationship that a natural, chronological diary makes apparent. In* The New Diary *dreams are kept as part of the spontaneous, ongoing record of personal evaluation. Dreams, memories, reflections, and the flow of your life all acquire meaning from their interconnections on the page.*

These days, since I'm more in tune with my tendency to write my dreams down, I not only recount them but also try to interpret them (more on that in a moment). For now, here are four dreams I was once compelled to write about. Each of these is a colorful illustration of what was going on in my mind at the time—except there is one that leans more toward the future. At the age of twenty-three, I had a dream about my wedding day. It may have been prophetic, or I may have walked by a Vera Wang store. You never know.

AT SIXTEEN

December 10, 1995

I had a dream last night and the details are a blur but I do know Mark was in it (Mark is the boy I met at Saranac Lake). Back to my dream. I was lying in a field wrapped in Mark's arms. I asked him if things were going to work this time or if he was going to forget me again. He said, "If a man's heart is not on his forehead then he'll hurt the two women he loves the most." There was another girl in my dream but I didn't know her.

AT EIGHTEEN

November 15, 1997

My father and I were minding Fergie* and Andrew's house. They lived in a house on the bay. It was rather small but there were two brick pillars in front indicating that royalty lived there. The only way to get to the house was by boat. My dad and I had one of those airplane slash boat devices. So one night Fergie, Andrew, their children, and my

*Referring to Sarah Ferguson, the Duchess of York, not Black Eyed Peas Fergie.

relatives were having a cocktail party. Fergie's girls started screaming about how they missed their auntie Dutch (that's what they used to call Diana*).

Then my father went out to get the boat and tried to fly it when one of the wings broke. There was a lot of smoke. That night I went to a dance and Gary was there. They started playing "Don't Cry for Me Argentina" and we danced. Then he pushed me (a good five feet) against the railing and began kissing me. I enjoyed it. Then I awoke suddenly.

AT TWENTY-THREE

March 10, 2003

I had an amazing dream last night. I dreamt I was at my wedding. I didn't realize I was getting married until I was pulled into the church. It was glorious. My dress was there—it was white and gold. Sounds tacky now, but then it was perfect. I asked if I could see my fiancé quickly before the ceremony. I ran into the sanctuary to see him—I had no idea who he was. A man my height with brown hair and glasses came toward me and embraced me in a most passionate way. He felt perfect. He told me how much he loved me and how he couldn't wait to marry me. I was filled with affection and love. I awoke before the ceremony began. I'm not looking to marry just yet, but that dream gave me a slight craving. I wonder if that man exists. I wonder if I'll ever find him.

*This was written two and a half months after Princess Diana died. I had a small obsession.

AT TWENTY-FOUR

December 20, 2003

I slept well last night—remarkably well. I didn't fear or ache. I did fall into a strange dream. A twister found its way to Manhattan. I saw the twister and watched it come close. It was powder white, and we (I remember seeing Jesse and Elise) were all running. The whole city was in a panic, and everywhere we ran was a beautiful room. As if the entire city had become some gorgeous Victorian castle. We ran up marvelous staircases and through ballrooms all to escape this twister. At one point I ran onto an estate where gentlemen where riding horses. They didn't know or care about the twister. Running from the twister had made me late for an editorial meeting on the top floor of the estate. The confer- ence room was filled with editors and the only one I recognized was Kate White.* I felt bad because I didn't have much to contribute to the meeting. Afterwards I left by way of a narrow staircase carpeted with red velvet and the halls were lit with candles. I love heavy sleep and heavy dreams.

EXPRESS YOUR
SUBCONSCIOUS SELF

I've recently altered the way I approach writing about dreams in my jour- nal. Where I once only retold the stories, I now delineate first and then take it a step further by trying to decipher what my subconscious was say- ing. This is the result of my attending a lecture series on Carl Jung (1875– 1961). The Swiss psychiatrist and founder of analytical psychology placed

*Editor in chief of *Cosmopolitan*.

great emphasis on understanding the psyche through exploring dreams. He believed dreams to be a conversation with the self. I've always enjoyed having dreams—makes sleep seem more worthwhile—and so I was game for digging in a little deeper.

- **Rise and Shine:** If you can, write your dreams down as soon as you wake up. This is when you will remember the minutia. Sometimes when I wake, I still feel like I'm in the dream, which makes for a more vivid recollection. If you don't get to it first thing, but it does occur to you at some other point during the day, still write it down. You may not remember as much, but you'll remember the big things. What you do remember can be very telling.

- **Self-interpretation:** By interpretation, I don't mean thumbing through those books that tell you dreaming about a burning cornfield means passion, or a waterfall means wealth. The dream came from you, which means the code is somewhere in you, too. Write about the dream and then try to decode it. If you think a symbol has more than one meaning, write all the possible meanings. Write what you want it to mean. Take note of how you felt in the dream versus how you'd normally feel if you were awake. For example, in the dream I had at eighteen, I included the small detail "I enjoyed it" when I mentioned kissing Gary. Gary was an acquaintance of mine who I never had any romantic interest in during my waking hours. Does that mean I was opening myself up to have romantic feelings for him? Or maybe he symbolized my enjoying something else in life I never thought I would. If an interpretation feels good, then go with it; if you're still perplexed, then that's fine, too. By writing, you're aligning the inner and outer you, and this might bring about more clarity in future dreams.

- **Talk to Your "Self":** This technique is hot off the presses (for me, anyway). It was suggested at the last Jungian lecture, and, as silly as I felt, I tried it. I wrote out a dream (it centered on a guy I was dating. Surprise!), then I offered my interpretation to the page, and I wrote a note to my Self. Literally. "Self: If you have any more insight into my feelings for or situation with Luke, I am ready and willing to receive. If you wish to tell me something else—about the upcoming year, perhaps—I am happy to receive that as well. This dialogue is open. Let's keep it that way."

I kid you not, I had dreams—or ones that I remembered, anyway—for the next five nights in a row. The follow-up dreams did not give me the insights or answers I wanted—they only served to confuse me more, but I think that's okay. I think my subconscious recognized my conscious willingness to try to figure out what was going on and challenged it with dream overload. Or maybe it was just my Self's way of telling me we have a long way to go before we fully understand each other. I know for sure that something was triggered. My plan is to keep writing and translating. My journey to the subconscious begins here.

PICTURE YOURSELF IN A BOAT ON A RIVER

To be completely honest, I have attempted to tap into my subconscious before—though, instead of relying on the natural dreamworld to do it, I took an artificial route. It began the day a group of us were smoking pot in the cow pasture (yes, that's really where we were). Marijuana had no effect on me that time or the subsequent times I tried it, so I shrugged my shoulders and figured it wasn't for me.

Drugs have always been the waking mind's back road to the sleeping mind—the conscious attempt to walk fully aware into the dreamworld. It's true not all drugs are hallucinogens, but they all offer an altered state of body and mind, and it is that promise of cerebral pleasure and temporary escape from reality that piques the curiosity of many. When I say many—I mean it. I don't know many people—and I'm willing to say you don't either—who haven't indulged in drugs in some way, shape, or form. Not that that makes it right. It just makes it so.

I discovered in my early twenties that even though marijuana wasn't for me, it didn't mean other artificial stimulants weren't. For someone who had never really smoked pot, going straight to cocaine was probably a little extreme. But I lived in Manhattan and that's the drug that was everywhere, so that's what I did. I was a social user. I wasn't addicted to the drug itself, but rather the drug in accordance with the lifestyle. I never craved it otherwise, but once I set foot inside a club, as soon as the music was too loud and the crowd overwhelming, I needed the adrenaline rush. This isn't to say what I was doing wasn't very foolish. It was. And this certainly isn't to say cocaine and its cohorts can't ruin lives. They can, and they show no partiality, whether it's in the rich and famous, the poor and destitute, or anyone in between. It just takes longer with some people than with others, and I became disillusioned before my habit became an addiction.

I didn't journal about my experimentation too often—I always thought about it, though. Any time I was high, I would think, *I can't wait to write about this,* and then I wouldn't. Or if I did end up writing, it always came out a lot less magnificent than it had been in my mind. The following are a few of my drug-induced musings. The first one is not from my journal, but rather is a short section of a novel I was working on—the main character, Cecilia, tries cocaine for the first time. Like many first novels, it was shamelessly autobiographical. I can see now that that personal project was crucial to my development as a writer, and it inadvertently served as an extension of my journal. I was repainting my friends, my living situation, my job, and myself in fictional colors. In order to do so, I had to step outside my small world and try to see things from different perspectives. The second entry denotes the drug Ecstasy, though it doesn't say it directly. The third entry is self-explanatory, and the last entry is from my sister's journal—she was fifteen when she wrote it. I had to include it so that I'm not the only one my mother gets mad at.

March 2003 (Excerpt from my novel)

Suddenly it felt as though Cecilia were breathing through her nose for the first time. The air was clean and cold, and she could feel the path leading from her nose to her brain—she didn't know there was one. Jimmy started talking again, but she wasn't paying attention. She felt possessed by an energy that sugar could never know. She was uninhibited and unafraid. She didn't realize she had finished her beer, but she looked down at the empty bottle and figured she must have. Her mouth was sticky and void of saliva. She was fidgety. She walked over to the balcony and placed both hands on the chilly marble surface—she leaned forward and didn't fear the fall. She breathed through her newly emancipated nose and looked down lovingly on the station's main concourse; she thought about how she'd like to run in and out of the columns before she went home.

October 12, 2003
I was rolling Friday
night — what an amazing
and frightening feeling.
All of the sudden I was
very aware of the fact
that my hips were moving
and that my skin was
still attached. And vienna
became my favorite scent
while lavendar was a
place I really wanted to
visit.

January 24, 2004

Time is still not on my side. Last night I had this all-consuming marijuana-induced craving for Tyler. I needed him to hold me. I was terrified. It was as though my mind were skipping. The same simple thoughts kept repeating themselves over and again. I feared I would spend the rest of my life in a trip—that trip was hell. No more drugs. I say that and can only hope I mean it.*

November 17, 1997 (My sister's entry)

I did the most bizarre thing today. I smoked pot and watched porn with Andy. Oddly, it got me hot, but now I feel really dirty and sorry. I feel weak and pitiful and very tired, so this won't be a long journal entry. I also saw *The Grinch*.

LEWIS CARROLL (1832–1898) ON USING YOUR DREAMS TO DEFINE INSANITY

Never have dreams and drugs come together in literature quite the way they do in *Alice's Adventures in Wonderland* and its sequel, *Through the Looking-Glass*. Charles Lutwidge Dodgson—the man we know and love by his pen name Lewis Carroll—was an author, a teacher, a photographer, and an avid diarist. He kept a diary his entire adult life, beginning at the age of twenty-one and ending in December 1896—less than a month before his death at the age of sixty-five.

Dodgson's diaries were consistent, straightforward, and usually

*The reason this high was unexpectedly traumatic—as marijuana doesn't usually affect me—was because I had taken Ritalin before smoking. Dumb.

A Self-portrait of Lewis Carroll.

short. He often elaborated on his dealings of the day and his swinging moods. Of the thirteen diaries that he amassed in his lifetime, only nine remain—four volumes were lost and ten pages from the surviving journals were torn out. The common assumption is that his family removed the material for reasons unknown, but that has yet to be proved.

In the existing diaries, there is nothing to suggest that Dodgson used drugs. However, it's difficult to believe that psychedelic substances had nothing to do with a smoking caterpillar and mushrooms that made Alice grow larger and smaller, and how about that Jabberwocky (can you say, "Bad trip"?) It is believed Dodgson may have taken laudanum—an opium preparation and the most common painkiller of the day—which was known to result in a high if a large enough dose was used. Regardless of the drug world, the dreamworld undoubtedly had a great deal of influence on *Alice*—as the entire adventure took place in Alice's dreams. The following journal entry was a quick thought Dodgson had on dreams five months before *Alice* was first published.

February 8, 1865

Query: when we are dreaming, and as often happens, have a dim consciousness of the fact and try to wake, do we not say and do things which in waking life would be insane? May we not then sometimes define insanity as an inability to distinguish which is the waking and *which the sleeping life? We often dream without the least suspicion of unreality: "Sleep hath its own world," and it is often as lifelike as the other. [This idea is, of course, developed in* Wonderland *since, as the Cheshire Cat informs Alice, "We're all mad here. I'm mad. You're mad."]**

*Annotation made by Roger Lancelyn Green, editor of The Diaries of Lewis Carroll.

CHAPTER 7

A DAY IN THE LIFE

Experience is what you get looking for something else.

—Mary Pettibone Poole

(Copied into my journal on April 30, 1999)

The human mind is expansive and inadequate all at once. We couldn't possibly remember the many minutes that make up our lives. A journal, if nothing else, is an excellent way to preserve some of the minutes that wouldn't stand a chance otherwise. We also forget about our former selves fairly easily, and it's good to go back and confront them every now and again. Naturally, we run the risk of recording bad judgments and mistakes, and what good is any life without bad judgments and mistakes? We also end up writing about the people, places, events, and, again, the minutes. The simple minutes that moved us for one reason or another. Sometimes the minutes that affect you are those that affect everyone—in the face of a national or global disaster—and your version of the story becomes part of the much larger picture. Then when you go, the journal lives on—if not for the world to read, then just for the people who love you and your descendants. In the book *How to Write:*

Advice and Reflections, author Richard Rhodes writes, "Only temples and pyramids enjoy such permanence as writing enjoys."

In high school, my journal was simply a sounding board for the emotional mishmash taking place. When I got to college, I started paying more attention to the outside world and tried drawing sketches and painting pictures with words. Here are a few of the minutes that have made up my life:

AT TWENTY

December 20, 1999

This morning I witnessed a father embrace his son. Last night at the orchestra I watched a young man suppress his boredom by vivaciously playing an imaginary violin. Absolutely precious! The world keeps me on constant tiptoes.

AT TWENTY-ONE

September 15, 2001

I've never taken pictures of the Empire State Building or the Statue of Liberty. Why would I? They'll always be there for me to look at. Same with the Flatiron Building and the World Trade Center. I can get on the subway and see them when I want. Right?

On Monday, September 10, the United States was innocent. Our problems were silly and selfish. We couldn't have known how vulnerable we were. On Tuesday morning two planes maliciously crashed into the Twin Towers and one into the Pentagon. The towers couldn't handle the heat and they both imploded. The city of New York along with the nation watched in horror. We are shocked and we are helpless.

I haven't worked all week. I tried to donate blood but to no avail. I feel empty. Now the talk of war is affecting me deeply. I went to work for the first time in four days. We had very few customers. They were playing this old music that sounded like the type played in World War II movies. I realized I might live to see the world at war again.

We don't see things as they are. We see them as we are.

~ Anaïs Nin, copied into my journal on October 19, 2006

AT TWENTY-TWO

April 19, 2002

I won't ever complain about being caught in the rain. It is a magnificent blessing. The sun was broad across the sky all day, but around 5:30 blue became gray and the sun slipped out of sight. I caught the subway and by the time I emerged from the ground the light gray sky had transformed into a brilliant black and orange spectacle. The buildings of Broadway looked artificial against this daunting backdrop. The wind pushed me along like an impatient mother behind her child. The rain pelted my back like small pieces of candy, and thunder, with his imminent partner, lightning, began their afternoon domination. It's always the first sign of summer—a righteous storm.

AT TWENTY-FIVE

April 27, 2005

This trip makes me hungry to see the rest of the world. We sit in the rocky, peaceful hills of Tepoztlán, Mexico. We're about an hour outside Mexico City where horses and dogs roam freely, the people are warm and lovely, and the landscape is breathtaking. There are not many tourists here. We've been given an honest glimpse into simple yet productive lives. This is almost the perfect vacation—we've climbed mountains, relaxed by the pool, eaten fun food, and walked through the colorful markets of Mexican life.

EXPRESS YOURSELF WITH A SPECIALTY JOURNAL

I once knew a girl who kept a strict day-in-the-life diary. I'd catch her writing on the dorm's common couch every now and again. She said she did it every day—wrote down what happened. From the distance at which I glanced over her shoulder, the entries never seemed to be longer than a page. She admitted there wasn't much detail included but rather a straightforward account of the day's occurrences. The fact that she did it fascinated me. Rereading the entries was probably a little on the boring side. It was as if she took a picture of herself every day—flipping through them would get old but having them all mounted on a massive wall at the end of her life would make for an awesome art exhibit.

Most of us (myself included) could never commit to such a thing. Many have a hard time committing even to a once-a-week journal, let alone the daily kind. If you aren't interested in a basic journal, I recommend keeping a journal of something that is of special interest to you. If the subject excites you, then you'll turn to write more often and will still manage to keep a compelling record of yourself. A few suggestions:

- **Travel Journal:** Traveling excites all the senses, and, yes, it's hard to write after a full day of exploration, but it's completely worth it. When I told a friend about this book, she said, "I always write a journal when I travel, and my traveling companions now expect a copy. So I have to censor myself a bit—and remember to note what they ate, too."

- **Book Journal:** You are what you read. If I'm at dinner party, the first place I usually go (I mean after the bar) is the bookshelves. You can tell so much about a person by way of what they read, and I like that insight into the host. You can also tell a great deal about yourself by the books you like and dislike. It's fun to be a critic, so write your own reviews, and be sure to copy down some of the lines that moved you the most.

- **Dream Journal:** If you don't care to write about your waking life but your "night" life fascinates you, dedicate a journal just to your dreams. The benefit of keeping dreams separate from a daytime diary is that you can see recurrent themes and imagery and this allows a more cohesive glimpse into your subconscious.

- **Restaurant Journal:** There is so much writing-worthy matter that comes together over a meal. Aside from the meal itself, you can describe the ambience, or lack thereof, as well as the people around and the conversation taking place. Many memories are made when breaking bread together.

- **Date Journal:** Seriously, why not? For the serial dater—write about and rate every guy or gal you go out with. Turn it into a blog (more on blogging in the next chapter).

A DAY IN THE LIFE OF THE PHILADELPHIA MUSEUM OF ART

As I was going through, I found several journal entries where I toted my pen and paper to the Philadelphia Museum of Art. It's still one of my fa-

vorite museums—I never get tired of going or of writing there—I just
didn't realize I had done it so many times. Each time I go, I search diligently for my favorite painting (it's never in the same place), which is described in two of the entries below. It's interesting to return periodically
and write in the same bustling space—you change, but the place, oftentimes, remains the same. You seek the familiarity with the hope of steady-
ing yourself. Or perhaps it's you who hasn't changed but the place has.
Either way, there is a new perspective to comprehend, and that's certainly
worthy of being written. Here are three of my art museum entries (the
third entry is a juicy one that concerns Tyler):

AT EIGHTEEN

January 1, 1998

My cousin Katie and I, along with my Aunt Kay, went to the Art
Museum today. There was an exhibit consisting of 250 dresses. I saw
so many colors and styles. I saw Princess Grace's wedding dress—it
was fading from white to a coffee-like color. She was very tiny and
especially elegant. I also saw a dress worn by none other than the late
Princess of Wales herself. I was truly enthralled. It was long and the
waist was small. I wanted to try it on so badly because I knew it
would fit.

AT NINETEEN

January 3, 1999

Life to Claude Monet seems windy. Well, by looking at his paintings
that's what I gathered. He preferred oil on canvas. The short strokes of
his brush place wind into each scene. Sometimes he paints a sweet

breeze and other times it's a vicious storm, like the one I awoke to. Monet experiments with colors.

In the paintings to my right I see a pastel candy factory, but in the painting directly in front of me I see the gloomy colors of the ocean. There is no particular mood in this room. The room itself is dull—it's the paintings and the people who bring it to life.

They say surrealism was brought on by psychology in the 1920s. Artists began an exploration of the human psyche using dream like images and fantasy settings. Please, Mr. Dali, tell me what you mean because I think I mean it too. Tell me all about snakes and spoons and feet in the mountain. I wish to know of faces in the wall and breasts in the floor.

My favorite picture in this "modern art" room is called Birthday. The setting is wooden and grey. It's a dream world. A girl stands at the front looking perplexed. Her skirt looks as though it's made of tablecloth and seaweed. Her shirt is open revealing two C sized very firm breasts and a washboard stomach. The seaweed is intertwined with her gray brown hair almost as though it is her hair. She is barefoot. Beside her is a flying monkey. His wings are extended but he is not preparing to take flight. He is searching for something, food perhaps.

AT TWENTY-SEVEN

December 31, 2006

I changed my mind as soon as I got here. On the walk over I wanted to turn around and go home, but now that I'm here it's not so bad. The lighting is good and the European Art, 1100–1500/Asian Art entrance still has the same intense statue of Jesus on the cross that it always has. I'm at the Philadelphia Art Museum. I'm home.

Since I last wrote I saw Tyler, told him I loved him, got a good initial response,* then didn't hear from him for a while, bought a house, heard from Tyler again in early December. Saw him on Friday, had sex with him (didn't mean to but was swept away). Being Tyler's sex on the side is easier than being anyone else's. He doesn't make me feel bad. He takes such good care of me. He tells me my naked body is gorgeous and asks again and again, "What can I do for you, Samara?"

I'm sitting here now still feeling him. Smelling him. The way soap scent sticks to his skin is amazing. He's amazing. I know I won't ever share this with anyone. But that's okay. I have loved to a greater degree in the past three years of being single than most people do in a long marriage. I'll tell Tyler soon I can't see him anymore. I'm just not ready yet. I want to savor him a little longer.

I haven't written in this journal in so long. I'm disappointed that it's been two years since I received it, and I'm not even halfway through. Perhaps journaling more often will be my New Year's resolution. I suppose some journals require more attention than others. If Tyler has anything to do with it I will write often and well. He'll forever be my muse.

Birthday, 1942, Oil on Canvas
Dorothea Tanning, American, Born 1910

I found her again. Not sure why I love this painting. I think it's the perfect doors and the perfect breasts.

*"Good initial response" means he e-mailed me the next day and we discussed where we were both coming from a bit further. He did not say, "I love you, too," nor did I expect him to.

SAMUEL PEPYS (1633–1703) ON A DAY IN THE LIFE OF A SEVENTEENTH-CENTURY ENGLISHMAN

Samuel Pepys—though not born into a noble family—managed to rise in the ranks and become both an English naval administrator and a member of Parliament. He is now most famous for the diary he kept between 1660 and 1669. Pepys (pronounced "peeps") wrote it in a form

Painting of Samuel Pepys by J. Haylls in 1666.

of shorthand from the period, so he probably intended the diary to be private. However, he thought to leave the book to his nephew and heir and, upon his nephew's death, to a library. He also left a key to the shorthand system, which, unfortunately, the first transcriber, the Reverend John Smith, didn't know about until it was too late. The diary, originally released in two volumes in 1825, is a candid juxtaposition of very personal events from Pepys's life (he writes openly about cheating on his wife) and his insights on politics and major events (he witnessed the Coronation of Charles II, the Great Plague (bubonic plague) of 1665, and the Great Fire of 1666. He stopped writing in his journal on May 31, 1669, due to failing eyesight. Here are a few days in his life in 1665:

January 4, 1665

Lay long, and then up to my Lord of Oxford's, but his Lordshipp was in bed past ten o'clock; and Lord help us! so rude a dirty family I never saw in my life. He sent me out word my business was not done, but should against the afternoon.

January 15, 1665 (Lord's Day)

Up, and after a little at my office to prepare a fresh draught of my vows for the next yeare, I to church, where a most insipid young coxcomb preached.

February 3, 1665

Up, and walked with my boy (whom, because of my wife's making him idle I dare not leave him at home) walked first to Salsbury court, there to excuse my not being home at dinner to Mrs. Turner. She was dressing herself by the fire in her chamber, and there took the occasion to show me her leg, which is indeed the finest I ever saw, and she is not a little proud of it.

June 20, 1665

This day I informed myself that there died four or five at Westminster of the plague in one alley several houses up Sunday last, Bell Alley, over against the Place-gate; yet people do think that the number will be fewer in the towne than it was last weeke.

✳ ✳ ✳

ALL THE NEWS THAT'S FIT TO BLOG

The first principle of a free society is an untrammeled
flow of words in an open forum.

—Adlai E. Stevenson

We are witnesses to the virtual evolution of a-day-in-the-life journals. They have gone public and manifested themselves into "an
opinion on the life," "a comment on the life," or "a tirade on the life." In
other words: a blog. For the longest time, I had no idea what a blog (the
marriage of the words *Web* and *log*) or blogger was. I'd watch CNN and
someone would say, "The Beltway bloggers are going crazy over this one."
Or on *E! News,* I'd hear, "The bloggers have not been kind to her these
past few weeks." I wondered if aliens were attacking us.

I eventually figured out that *blogger* was just another word for a person
who keeps an online diary. A blog might resemble a diary entry literally,

where one spills about what one did over the weekend, or it could lean more toward the op-ed style of asserting political views. A blog could be perceptive and brilliant or hackneyed and boring, and you, as the reader, are welcome to let the writer know just what you think of the blog. I was a little disappointed at first because, by the way news programs talk, I was expecting not bloggers but wizards. But I had overlooked the obvious value. With blogs, every person is entitled to a virtual place of their own. We, the people, can publish opinions, launch campaigns, write to-do lists, rant, and rave, all at a minimal expense. Web sites once lent to this, too, but blogs go further and encourage readers to add comments—creating open and sometimes impassioned forums.

There is mounting pressure to be a blogger these days (I hesitate to say that because by the time this book comes out, we could be over blogs and on to the next thing). For now, however, it's true. It's not enough to have just a magazine or a newspaper anymore—publications have to reach readers on the blogging level. Just about everyone has one—musicians, writers, actors, video game enthusiasts, and anyone else with a Web site. Some have gone so far as to scrap the whole Web site and just have a blog. If *Sex and the City* had run for just one more season, Carrie Bradshaw would have had to expand her column into a blog. I'm curious to see if they'll give her one in the movie.

I resisted blogging wholeheartedly at first, but I resist most technological advancements at first. It took me years to get a cell phone, I still don't have a BlackBerry, and I only set up MySpace and Facebook profiles within the past few months. I'm like the Amish in that I like to watch inventions do their thing from afar and make sure they won't upset my world before I decide to participate. Anyway, I revamped my Web site in early 2007 and reluctantly included a blog. I just didn't know what the point of it would be and feared my random musings wouldn't be of interest to anyone. Before the site relaunched, I decided that the blog would have to be about letter writing, because that was the theme of the site.

Letter writing came up in the world more often than I expected it to, and I began to warm up to the practice of blogging. It was a new creative outlet—more organized than a journal entry and less structured than a full-on article. However, like a journal entry, length didn't matter, which is a favorite feature of mine. I, like many infant bloggers, had to deal with the fact that no one was commenting on my blog, but I kept at it nonetheless.

In September 2007, I began blogging for the *Huffington Post.* The *HuffPo* is a sign of the times if ever there was one. It's an online-only newspaper made up of 1,800 bloggers (it'll be more by the time you read this), who offer their opinions on everything you can think of. I really began to have a blast with blogging when I started writing for them. A blog is posted no matter what, but if it's well liked by the editor, then it's put on the front page of your section (as of now, I write for the "Living" section). This was incentive for me to be as inventive with my blogs as possible. By far, my favorite journal-like quality of blogs is that they go unedited. Whether I post on my own blog or on the *Huffington Post,* my words are not changed. Of course, I have to suffer the consequences and take credit for any and all mistakes, but for writers, it is a gift to have works published completely unaltered.

It is my hope that bloggers are printing their blogs or filing them in some other secure way, so this medium reserves its spot in history. Blogs are the quintessential testament to a day in the life of the early twenty-first century. As we now skim the shelves and see books such as *The Diary of Virginia Woolf, 1925–1930,* our descendants may buy *The Unabridged Blogs of Perez Hilton* (Oh, Lord, what will our offspring think?). My *Huffington* blogs are on the lengthier side, so here are a few short ones I wrote for my private blog. The first is a letter I sent to the *New York Times* that wasn't published—making it an automatic blog. These appear in reverse chronological order as they do online.

LETTER TO THE *NEW YORK TIMES* EDITOR

August 1, 2007

With regards to the article: <u>IN THE '60s, A FUTURE CANDIDATE POURED HER HEART OUT IN LETTERS by MARK LEIBOVICH</u> (July 29):* Thank you for the glimpse into the collegiate dalliances and uncertainties of Hillary Clinton through the letters she wrote to John Peavoy. The snippets shown (I regret but understand that they were not able to be reprinted in their entirety) offer access to the refreshingly unpolished thoughts of a young woman even Mrs. Clinton doesn't know anymore. That is the beauty of letters—they capture the musings of the moment but last a lifetime and beyond. We may very well be witnessing the last generation to have their stories told in their own words through letters. This is tragic. Without leaving tangible, eloquent evidence of ourselves, our descendants will think our lives were as emotionally void as our IMs and MySpace pages—which have yet to prove staying power. And if our online profiles ultimately expire, then what honest portraits of daily life have we painted?

Posted in *Historical Letters, Letters in the News* | *No Comments »*

HANDWRITING OF THOSE LONG GONE

JULY 11, 2007

I was at a wedding this past weekend and ended up speaking with a friend of a friend about my book. Toward the tail end of the conversation

* Links to the *New York Times* article.

he said, "Isn't it sad how our handwriting has suffered greatly because no one writes letters anymore?" Although I purport there have been a great many losses as a result of the lack of letters in today's world, I don't think handwriting is one of them. I tried to explain to him that Edgar Allan Poe had horrible handwriting and when I see scans of his letters online I am grateful that I'm not the one who had to transcribe them. He was still skeptical, saying, "I'm not so sure about that . . ." Lo and behold! Robert Fisk of the *Independent* comes to my rescue today in an amusing piece about <u>the horrible handwriting of those who have gone before</u>.* Today's lesson: Don't be embarrassed by your penmanship—write letters anyway. Someone will take the time to transcribe them someday.

Posted in *Historical Letters, Letters in the News* | *2 Comments* »

LETTER WRITERS OF THE WORLD UNITE FOR . . . PARIS HILTON?

June 21, 2007

Whatever it takes to get people writing letters, I suppose. I am usually not an outspoken advocate for the elder Hilton sister, but in this case I applaud her for giving her father a handwritten note for Father's Day and for following it up a few days later with a <u>thank-you note</u>** to the scores of people who have written her while in jail. The queen of T-Mobile has brought out the inner letter writer in hundreds of fans as well as the Duchess of York (can we still call her that?). <u>Sarah Ferguson</u>,*** too, wrote a sympathetic letter to Paris earlier this week offering her support. Now, if Paris continues sending thoughtful handwritten notes

*Links to the *Independent* (British publication) article.
**Links to Paris's letter.
***Links to an article about Sarah Ferguson's letter.

to her fans when she gets out of jail, then may lightning strike me if I say another bad word about her.

Posted in <u>Letters in the News</u> | <u>1 Comment »</u>

KATIE AND TOM DO SOMETHING WRITE!

June 14, 2007

. . . Well, Katie did something right anyway. According to this week's *People* magazine Katie Holmes and daughter Suri were shopping in the Ladies in Waiting children's store in Shreveport, La.—where Katie is filming the upcoming *Mad Money*—and the shop owners gave Suri a pink picture frame with her name on it. In response to the thoughtful gift, Katie sent the boutique a thank-you note on "Suri Cruise" personalized stationery. Katie has her daughter off to a good start in the way of manners and meaningful gestures.

Posted in <u>Letters in the News</u> | <u>No Comments »</u>

EXPRESS YOURSELF ONLINE

A blog can be about anything and everything. For as many book topics as there are in the world, so there are blog subjects. Not only can you publish your journal online, but you can also comment on global warming or the stale coffee you drank this morning—you can even give hourly updates on your beloved hamster. Your imagination is the limit.

- **Blog About Your Likes and Dislikes:** If you ever find yourself saying, "I hate it when . . ." or "I like it when . . ." then that makes for good blogging material. I hate it when people count change in line at the grocery store. I hate it when boys don't call back. I hate that album. I hate Britney as a brunette. I do, however, like Christina as a brunette. I like it when guys open car doors. I really like that movie. And I like to tip the girl who bags my groceries. Elaborate on what it is about that thing you like or dislike, and there you have it. My last *Huffington* blog was about how much it bothers me when people don't R.S.V.P. I would never go so far as to elaborate on that in my journal nor would I turn it into an entire article. Therefore, it's a blog.

- **React in Your Blog:** Blogs are great for gut reactions. If an article you read recently infuriated you, write a letter to the editor. If the editor doesn't print it, then post it in your blog. Assert your opinion on the latest celebrity gossip. Respond to local or national events. Chances are if you're feeling a certain way about something that happened in your community, someone else is feeling that way, too. Putting it out there can bring like-minded people together. It can also start a heated debate. That's okay—this is what the forum is for.

- **Don't Forget to Link:** If you are reacting to an article, photo, book, or another blog, be sure to hyperlink your blog to that source. You've shared your reaction, now give viewers the chance to hone in and react for themselves. This is one of the reasons the Web is remarkable—information sources are feeding off one another like never before.

- **Give Your Blog a Theme:** A themed blog will undoubtedly bring compatible people together and make you an expert on whatever topic you choose. At first, I felt peer-pressured into blogging on my Web site, but once I decided to stick with the theme and follow it in as many directions as possible, I felt like my blog had a purpose and I wasn't as much of a sellout. Whatever you're passionate about is what will inspire you to blog regularly. Here are the sites of a few fun themed blogs I've found (disclaimer: These are active at the present time—they might not always be):

- soulofstartrek.blogspot.com

- pez-blog.com

- saturday-morning-cartoons.blogspot.com

- reducecellulite.blogspot.com

- **Remain Anonymous:** The beauty (sometimes the ugly) of the Web is that you can remain completely anonymous. If you want to launch a daring, risqué, or ideologically controversial blog, then the option is certainly open. Even if the topic isn't especially bold, but you want the words to be the star of the show rather than the writer, or you want to test your skills as a writer without opening yourself up to direct finger pointing, then this is a good way to go.

- **Consider Yourself Warned:** People aren't always nice and they can and will leave negative, sometimes really mean, comments on your blog. Porn sites will definitely leave dirty messages. As the one who runs the blog, you have to approve the comments before they are posted, but you will see all of the comments regardless. They can hurt your feelings or gross you out whether you post them or not. Try to make your peace with not taking things personally before you launch your blog. Such criticism is not always easy, but it's a small price to pay for having an outlet for your opinion.

ON BEING BLOGGED ABOUT

If you live on the planet Earth in the early twenty-first century, then you are at risk—at all times and in all places—of being blogged about. Some people are, naturally, in more danger than others. If you've won an Oscar, worked in the Oval Office, had a sex tape distributed globally, or all of the above, your chances are much greater. However, the rest of us are still at risk, whether we know someone with a blog or not. Strangers, lovers, friends, and enemies might see you as the perfect subject for their online ramblings. If you enlighten an acquaintance or offend a passerby, you're a contender. If you cut down your neighbor's sassafras tree while he's on vacation—yup, you guessed it—you've just nominated yourself for his blog. If you break someone's heart, oh, baby, you're getting *blogged* about.

My ex-boyfriend, Jesse, is a stand-up comedian (*jessejoyce.com*). Comedians tend to use their blogs to publish material that they've decided isn't quality enough for the stage but still warrants a laugh out loud. If you do or say anything dumb within five feet of a comedian, it will be publicly scrutinized. The thing is, you might never know. You may have no idea there is a comedian in the room, and he or she won't necessarily go so far as to ask for your name. You'll simply be referred to as "the guy wearing green spandex and a top hat at the CVS in downtown Toledo."

I've been blogged about both anonymously and by name. An anonymous blog looks like this one my friend Astrid (*huffingtonpost.com/ rev-astrid-storm*) wrote: "At a recent dinner with friends, someone at the table recalled a conversation she had with an Episcopal priest. . . ." Oh! Oh! It's me! It's me! I'm the "someone at the table." The first time I was blogged about by name was in February 2006. I met a wonderful woman on a press trip and ended up telling her about my letter-writing Web site, which she found very interesting. She had launched an inspirational blog (*waynesworld2005.blogspot.com*),* to count down the days until her son Wayne, who was serving in Iraq, would be home. He's safe and sound now. My Web service and I made the cut. She opened the blog with "The only thing bigger than Samara O'Shea's smile is her heart." Isn't that sweet? I thought that was sweet. Thank you, Rebecca!

I recently found one of the more amusing blogs I've read about myself. It was written a few months ago, but I only just found it because—okay, we're all adults here, I'll say it—I was Googling myself. I came across a review of my first book at *booksarepretty.blogspot.com*.* Needless to say, I'm a huge fan of book-review blogs. Keep up the good work, guys! The reviewer didn't like my title (I appreciate the honesty), but liked the book, and made many kind comments. The reviewer was not a fan, however, of my letter-writing service. She (or he, the blogger is anonymous) wrote, "However, if it's a love letter you're wanting to write, please don't hire her. Do it yourself, or don't do it at all." The person goes on to state the reason: "To be perfectly blunt, O'Shea doesn't want to blow your boyfriend. You do. And no matter how skilled the writer, that kind of passion is very, very hard to fake." Long live bluntness! I loved this, but I can't make any promises—I haven't met your boyfriend.

THOMAS PAINE (1737–1809) ON BEING AN EFFECTIVE PAMPHLETEER

Before there was the blogger, there was the pamphleteer (please note: an equally ridiculous word). If you had access to a printing press and an

---

*Same deal here—I don't know that these Web sites will be around forever.

Thomas Paine oil painting
by Auguste Millerè (1880).

important message too short for a book and too long for a newspaper, a pamphlet it was. One of the more distinguished pamphleteers in American history was political theorist Thomas Paine. He was born in England and emigrated to the American colonies in 1774 at the age of thirty-seven. He worked as the managing editor of *Pennsylvania Magazine* for a short time. As tensions began to mount between the colonies and Great Britain, Paine first called for reconciliation. After the Battle of Lexington and Concord, however, he became a staunch advocate for separation. In early 1776, Paine anonymously published the pamphlet *Common Sense*—the first relentless assault on the principles of monarchy. He called for the colonies to declare independence. The philosophical pamphlet went on to explain how a government could be effectively run by the people, and also how the upper and lower classes could share in both responsibility and privilege. It spread quickly, was well received throughout the colonies, and added abundant fuel to the revolution. Naturally, there were a few naysayers—notably a loyalist named James Chalmers, who published a rebuttal pamphlet called *Plain Truth*. *Common Sense* stands today as testament to the value of and need for freedom of expression. The work is divided into five sections. This is the introduction:

Philadelphia, Feb. 14, 1776

Perhaps the sentiments contained in the following pages, are not YET sufficiently fashionable to procure them general favor; a long habit of not thinking a thing WRONG, gives it the superficial appearance of being RIGHT, and raises formidable outcry in defense of custom. But the tumult soon subsides. Time makes more converts than reason.

As a long and violent abuse of power is generally the means of calling the right of it in question, (and in matters too which might never have been thought of, had not the sufferers been aggravated into the inquiry,) and as the king of England hath undertaken in his OWN RIGHT, to support the parliament in what he calls THEIRS, and as the good people of this country are grievously oppressed by the combination, they have an undoubted privilege to inquire into the pretensions of both, and equally to reject the usurpations of either.

In the following sheets, the author hath studiously avoided every thing which is personal among ourselves. Compliments as well as censure to individuals make no part thereof. The wise and worthy need not the triumph of a pamphlet; and those whose sentiments are injudicious or unfriendly, will cease of themselves, unless too much pains is bestowed upon their conversion.

The cause of America is, in a great measure, the cause of all mankind. Many circumstances have, and will arise, which are not local, but universal, and through which the principles of all lovers of mankind are affected, and in the event which, their affections are interested. The laying a country desolate with fire and sword, declaring war against the natural rights of all mankind, and extirpating the defenders thereof from the face of the earth, is the concern of every man to whom nature hath given the power of feeling; of which class, regardless of party censure, is

The Author

CHAPTER 9

CRIMES OF PASSION

When choosing between two evils,
I always like to try the one I've never tried before.

—Mae West

Spilt-second decisions are dangerous. They take no time to make, but the results can last a lifetime—especially if the decision isn't actually made by you, but rather by your anger, greed, lust, revenge, or insatiable appetite. And yet, there's something sweet about them, isn't there? There's something invigorating about a decision that just makes itself. In the moment, it feels both inappropriate and incredible. You suffer a temporary fever. Then if someone—it could even be you—ends up getting hurt, physically or emotionally, that passion, which was so pressing at the time, abandons you and you're left stranded to explain yourself. Some choose not to write about crimes of passion in their journals because it's too risky. It's undeniable evidence that a stealthy person could easily access. Others choose not to write because they don't want to acknowledge what they're doing even to themselves. Writing makes everything real and without putting your actions on paper it's easier to live in denial.

I don't know if they're the two most frequent crimes of passion, but the two that come to mind first are murder and cheating (on your significant other, that is). Since I, thankfully, don't know any murderers, this chapter will deal exclusively with cheating (well, except for the presidential assassination at the end). Shamefully, the first one to own up to this crime will be me. Yes, I was twenty-two years old and restless in a two-year relationship. Instead of discussing my concerns with the man who had been nothing but wonderful to me, I turned to a man who was pompous and inconsiderate (we had a lot in common). He, too, was cheating on his girlfriend. What a couple of winners we were. Let me tell you. The way my boyfriend, Jesse, found out I was cheating on him (oh, the irony)—he read my journal.

You may be wondering what compelled me to journal about cheating. I wonder that myself. I remember doing it. I was sitting in the downtown Manhattan DMV with at least a forty-five minute wait in front of me, so I opened my journal and spilled dirty details all over the page. The best answer I can offer is, I tell my journal everything. Why *wouldn't* I write about it is the more relevant question. If I had a therapist, surely I would have to tell him or her that I was cheating. The issue of "What problems do you see in your relationship?" can't really be addressed otherwise. I felt as safe writing about it as I would have telling a psychiatrist—never fearing for a second that Jesse would read it.

I must be clear in saying that Jesse was not that ever-doubtful type of boyfriend. He didn't have my voice mail access code or my e-mail password, nor had he ever asked for them. He never cared to spy or check up on me. He went into my journal because, to his credit, he knew me very well, and he sensed that something was very wrong. He confronted me twice. The first time, he asked me what was wrong. I answered, "Nothing." The second time, he asked me if there was someone else. I said no. He knew better and rightfully sought evidence to support his unwelcome theory.

The thing about lying on top of cheating is you convince yourself that you're doing the other person a huge favor. You think you're saving them all this emotional agony, when in reality you're prolonging it. You've checked out of the relationship emotionally if you've seen fit to put your passion elsewhere, and your boyfriend, girlfriend, husband, or wife suffers as a result of that whether they know you're cheating or not. It's one thing to walk in the door and say, "Hi, honey. I've been cheating on you!" I can understand not doing that, especially if you've decided to end the affair. But if and when you're confronted, it's because the other person senses the disconnect (or has happened upon a pair of panties in the glove compartment), and you (meaning me) owe them the truth. If I had really been considering Jesse's feelings, I wouldn't have been cheating at all; the lying only served to protect my pathetic self. Not to mention, cheating should have been a big, bad red flag in my own mind. By my actions, I was, in effect, yanking myself aside and saying, "*Psst!* Something is wrong with the relationship." But I completely ignored myself and was content to feign that everything was fine.

On the surface, I'm sure the takeaway from this story, aside from not cheating at all, is not to write about cheating in your journal, but if you're an avid journaler, you can't afford not to—not writing about it may very well mean that you're in denial. Lying to another person is bad, but lying to yourself about lying to another person is torment—no good can come of it. If you can, write not only about the cheating but also about why you're cheating—make yourself figure out exactly why you're doing it. Do a better job of hiding your journal than I did, but at least come clean to yourself. If you don't plan to stop cheating, which I didn't, then you should confess to the other person. If you do plan to stop, you can use your journal to help put the affair to bed, both in your mind and in actuality. The next step is figuring out whether you want your partner to know. On the one hand, it's considered selfish to fess up to such a thing because you're assuaging your own guilt. On the other hand, the truth shall set you free. If you decide not to tell, I still suggest writing about it—burn the pages or put your diary in a safe-deposit box when it's all over, but look your actions in the eye.

The good news was, I wasn't lying to myself about what was going on. The bad news was, I was lying to my significant other about it. The lesson learned, for me, was that in the end, I figured out the source of the problem and that in future relationships, I can address it long before it gets to the cheating point. In retrospect, I'm glad Jesse read my journal. Sometimes I think the better part of me motivated the worse part of me to write about what I was doing. I (bad angel) was too inconsiderate to tell him, and I (good angel) found a way to tell him so that he could make his decision accordingly. When the evidence is written in someone else's hand, then there's still a little room for lying—blaming the other person for having the wrong idea or simply saying, "It only happened once. It ended months ago!"—but when it's written in your own hand with a date on it, then there are no lies left to tell. This, in a way, is good. Jesse, justly, ended the relationship immediately, and I didn't fight it. As a matter of fact, it wasn't until it ended officially that I realized how overdue the ending really was. Here you'll find two of the incriminating journal entries that Jesse read, followed by the one I wrote after it all went down.

AT TWENTY-TWO

February 19, 2002

C'est la vie! Would someone explain to me why deception is so appealing and why I am not? I'll always be silly enough to try and accommodate them. Them being the inconsiderate and ill intentioned. I suppose I am one of them now . . . never considering Jesse and the way he feels. I'm always thirsty for trouble.

I haven't been able to stay away from Stephen. His compliments are too appealing. For those 35-minutes he is flawless. He thrusts like it's a mission, and I won't ever be able to articulate the way he tosses me around like a lascivious rag doll. I imagine this makes me a freshman again. Wait! I'm not done. I hope he (Stephen) turns me into a man. A man with little to no feelings—I just want to be desensitized to those who are desensitized to me.

February 21, 2002

I was so pleased with myself. I overcame Stephen . . . I set him aside and was ready for the next sardonic challenge (sardonic may have been the wrong word to use here . . . but it felt good). Then one Saturday night after downing several glasses of Pinot Noir he confessed his attraction for me. Now, I want more than the physical with him but the carnivore inside me is willing to settle for just that. So we praised, rubbed, and feasted on each other's bodies for about an hour, but the wine wouldn't allow him to complete the phase. I accepted the night as an invitation to another night—a night where we would complement and complete each other's needs.

(And after Jesse read my journal . . .)

March 1, 2002

Forgive me father for I have sinned again and again and again and again. Jesse's hands sought out and read my journal . . . (the entry on the page before this one probably hurt the most). I know now that I have the power to hurt others. He was the one person who deserved it the least. He deserved nothing but devotion. I allowed my desires to take over. I wanted them to take over. I wanted to live a life of constant passion. The trouble of it. The feeling of it. I didn't give Jesse the steadfast love he deserved. I was amazingly selfish. I was ready for our relationship to return to friendship, but this was the most horrific way to do it. My mind has been interrupted. I'm not sure what's going on.

HOW TO MAKE A JOKE
OUT OF YOUR GIRLFRIEND'S
CHEATING ON YOU

There were actually a few more journal entries about Stephen that I don't have in me to show. I haven't set eyes on those write-ups in five years, and revealing the ones I included here was harder than I thought it would be. As you can imagine, there was a showdown. Jesse and I both cried a lot. He told me I had succeeded in my mission to become "inconsiderate and ill-intentioned," and he was right. The next few weeks were stressful and emotionally exhausting, and then we became friends. It is a forgiveness feat I still marvel at—one that I can only hope I could extend. We started off as friends, so returning to that place wasn't easy considering the circumstances, but it was possible, and we've been at it ever since. We've known each other for ten years—two of those were the dating years. I think we both realized how much better off we were as friends, and this was the unfortunate event that led us to that conclusion. I'm grateful that the universe taught me this lesson—that selfishness of this sort is beyond unacceptable—and still allowed me to keep my best friend.

I am a great ex-girlfriend, by the way. I am the Jimmy Carter of ex-girlfriends. I have put much effort into Jesse's career as a stand-up comedian and have been there in the wake of other girls gone wrong. He, too, is an outstanding ex and has aided me in my career and listened to my many dating woes. Sometime in 2005 (three years after "the incident"), he called me and said, "I wrote a joke about you."

"Is it about my mother?" I asked. He had been threatening to do a joke about my mother forever.

"No, it's about you cheating on me."

"Oh, okay," I said, having no idea what the appropriate reaction was.

Not that there was ever much doubt in my mind, but if I had wondered whether or not he really forgave me, I knew in that moment he had. Like any skilled artist, he took the pain and made it work for him. He took our story to the stage:

> *[Bit about one of my other ex-girlfriends] . . . The girlfriend before her, she cheated on me. I knew she was cheating on me and I kept asking her about it and she wouldn't tell me the truth, so I know this isn't cool, ladies, but I had to read her journal. [At this point, women in the audience will usually gasp at the indiscretion, in which case I will remind them that "we could also focus on the part about her cheating on me. That is also very uncool."]*
>
> *But here's the problem: As painful as that thing was to read, she's an author, so that journal was REALLY well written. I was like, "Man, this is a fuckin' page-turner. I wonder if this dude's gonna find out she's cheating on him," which I guess is better than me reading her journal and her being a BAD writer. That would just piss me off on a whole other level, "Oh my God, that's another run-on sentence, whore!"*

EXPRESS YOURSELF BEFORE THE CRIME IS COMMITTED

Crimes of passion are arguably subconscious decisions. Not to the point where you'd kill someone in your sleep—though I'm sure that's happened—but where a powerful part of you does move to sin without consulting the rest of you. One way we learn not to be rash is through experience—action and reaction. As a minor, letting your anger get the best of you and punching Drake Connors could result in detention. As an adult, it can result in his pressing charges, and hopefully we learn to rein in our rage before it comes to anything like that. Another way we can start to face what's going on in our subconscious is by writing down those absurd thoughts that we're surprised cross our minds—*I felt the sudden urge to strangle her!* or *Kissing him would be so easy. No one would have to know.* It takes a lot of courage to write such things, but it helps you to confront your potential impulses before you act on them.

Once the two levels of consciousness are in cahoots, then split-second decisions can have the same outcome as well-thought-out decisions. I'm not there yet, by the way, and I don't know many people who are. Yoda and Mr. Miyagi are the only two I can think of who have gotten to this evolved state of mind.

- **As Soon as You Think of It:** Write down those fleeting thoughts that you'd prefer didn't just occur to you. You can normally look back and see in retrospect when a crime of passion started to take place, and it's usually well before it actually happens. As soon as you feel yourself attracted to your boyfriend's best friend, as soon as you realize how easy it would be to fiddle with that woman's parachute, or as soon as you decide it would be effortless to get your crush drunk and sleep with him while you're ovulating (did I say that out loud?), write it down. Look at it. You thought of it, therefore in some alternate universe you are capable of it. Just know that the thought is real, and line up your moral minutemen so they're ready to go when you call them.

- **Consider the Consequences:** If a temptation, such as cheating, is really getting the better of you, write out the possible scenario. Seriously consider the consequences. List the people (including yourself) who would get hurt and to what degree they could be burned. What relationships are at stake if you go through with it? Is it really worth the risk? If no, what situations can you avoid so you don't place yourself directly in temptation's way?

- **To Hell with the Consequences:** There are some moments in life when we decide to treat ourselves to a heaping spoonful of selfishness. We've weighed the consequences and say, "You know what? I'm still doing it, and I'm doing it for me." There are benefits to these moments, too. You could unleash a passion that has been cooped up for far too long, and it ultimately tells you about yourself and your hidden desires. Or you could get caught in the act and end up with a lesson learned for life. You could also survive by the skin of your teeth and live to commit many more crimes of passion. Whatever the outcome, be sure to write these down, too. They'll make your journal more scandalous and ultimately more interesting.

THE DANGERS OF FORGIVING TOO SOON

Let it be known that I am a staunch advocate of the act of forgiveness—in any and every circumstance. Naturally, it's not always easy, but it is always necessary. Forgiveness has been extended to me in many cases where I did not deserve it, and who am I not to grant others the same. I firmly believe that if you don't forgive someone, then that person wins—they get to keep tight hands around your throat. In her compelling best seller *Traveling Mercies: Some Thoughts on Faith,* author Anne Lamott writes, "In fact, not forgiving is like drinking rat poison and waiting for the rat to die." Exactly! The caustic chemicals swirl all around inside—making you an increasingly bitter person. It hurts my heart when I hear people say, "I will *never* forgive him!" I can understand not being able to forgive someone immediately after the fact, but setting out to never forgive someone is like inviting elephants to sit on your shoulders for the rest of your life. And, yes, forgiveness is difficult. If it were easy, then there would be no lessons learned or personal transformation taking place. There have been incidents in my life when pardoning someone seemed impossible, but through the process of passing my vitriol on to my journal, I was able to come around.

All that being said, forgiveness can take time. I remember an episode, and my journal confirmed it for me, where I was the victim of a crime of passion and forgiving too soon did more harm than good. My junior year of high school, my best friend, Clara, dated my ex-boyfriend, Shawn, less than a month after he broke up with me. I was understandably livid. I forgave her quickly, though, for two reasons: The first reason was, I didn't want to divide our group of friends right down the middle. The second reason was, I wanted to show her and everyone else that I was the bigger person (read the last part of this sentence in the most pompous voice you can). That's what I wanted. I wanted to be praised for being able to forgive someone for such a horrible act. The problem was, I didn't really forgive her. I pretended I did and then found six thousand not-so-subtle ways to remind her what a bad friend she was. At one point, Shawn stopped calling her, (he eventually started again) and I saw that as an opportunity to pounce.

July 16, 1995

Friday night, Megan, myself, and Mike slept over Anna's. At around 11 p.m. the four of us called Shawn. Anna and I were looking for a ride to a party the next day and his name came up. When we called we decided to give him a little guilt trip about not calling Clara. Shawn answered the phone and Mike said, "Call Clara," in a ghostlike voice. Shawn said, "Who is this?" and Mike answered, "Your conscience."

The next morning we called Clara only to find out Shane called her (thinking it was Clara). She wasn't too happy. I called her house today and left a message, but she hasn't called back yet. It frustrates me to think that she wouldn't be able to forgive me for something so small and stupid after I forgave her for going out with Shawn. She wouldn't be crying over him if she hadn't done that to me in the first place.

Oh, how I miss prank-calling people, but that's not the point. The point is, I was being a bitch, and I was lying to myself in my journal. Of course, Shawn thought Clara called him. That's what we set out to do—embarrass her. I instigated the whole thing, and then I put my hands on my hips and said, "She better not even think about not forgiving me!" You can't forgive someone and then rub it in that person's face that you forgave them. That's mal-forgiveness. I was clearly still hurting, and I wanted to make sure Clara knew it. A few days later, I was more honest with myself:

July 22, 1995
It's too late, I can't get mad anymore. I already forgave and oh how I wish I didn't. How could she do this to me? She's so weak. She couldn't say no if her life depended on it. She lies just to spare other people's feelings. That bitch even lies to Shawn. What a great way to start off a relationship. Yes, I'm talking about my wonderful friend Clara who said, "I can't hurt you, Samara," but then proceeded to go out with Shawn. This happened about a month ago and sometimes I don't care but sometimes I ~~hate~~ dislike her.

This more direct journal entry opened me up, and, for the next few weeks, I wrote on and on about Clara and how distressed I was because of what she had done. At one point, I even went so far as to write that I wished she'd get pregnant and that that would *show* "little Miss Perfect." That was a mighty vindictive thought, but it was a thought my anger led me to, so I wrote it. Owning up to my journal also made me realize how jealous I was, and had always been, of Clara. Standing silently in front of that fact was difficult, but it was also the beginning of getting over it. I did continue to befriend her, but revenge-inspired incidents became fewer and fewer. It's true I wasn't dealing with my resentment directly to Clara's face, but, by writing, I was still dealing with it. I knew that I wanted to forgive and forget, but I couldn't flip a switch and make that happen, so in the meantime, I placed my pain on paper. Looking back, I shouldn't have been so quick to "forgive" Clara. I was hurt and betrayed, and I needed to let those emotions run their course. Sometimes a gash has to bleed for a while before the healing can begin. Only when I no longer felt the need to make her feel bad should I have motioned to befriend.

In due time, I was able to legitimately forgive Clara. Our senior year, the school librarian dubbed the two of us *hippies* because we were attached at the hip. Then came college, and we drifted far apart. Today, we are friends on Facebook. When I think of Clara now, all I think of is how much fun we had and how much I loved her. If I hadn't written about the Shawn thing, there's a chance I might have forgotten it. All of the negativity from that situation went into my journal, and that's where it stayed.

JOHN WILKES BOOTH (1838–1865) ON HOW TO JOURNAL AFTER YOU JUST KILLED THE PRESIDENT

At the age of twenty-six, John Wilkes Booth was an accomplished actor and a Confederate sympathizer. He was upset over the South's defeat in the Civil War, but it was Lincoln's plan to grant suffrage to the freed slaves that infuriated him. Blinded by his rage, Booth led a group of co-conspirators in a plot to kill Abraham Lincoln and Secretary of State William Seward—with the hope of sending the Union into upheaval and ideally enabling the South to reorganize its war efforts. Only Booth was successful in carrying out his plan. He shot Lincoln on Good Friday, April 14, 1865, at Ford's Theatre in Washington, D.C. As a renowned actor, Booth was a friend of the owner of Ford's Theatre, John Ford, and

John Wilkes Booth in his acting heyday.

given access to all parts of the venue without suspicion. Following the assassination, Booth escaped to southern Maryland and continued on to a farm in northern Virginia. He was eventually tracked down and executed by Union soldiers on April 26. Found on him was a small red book—an 1865 appointment book—he used as a diary during his twelve days on the run.

April 1865

Until to-day nothing was ever thought of sacrificing to our country's wrongs. For six months we had worked to capture; but our cause being almost lost, something decisive and great must be done. But its failure was owing to others, who did not strike for their country with a heart. I struck boldly, and not as the papers say. I walked with a firm step through a thousand of his friends, and was stopped, and pushed on. A colonel was at his side. I shouted "Sic Semper Tyrannis!"* before I fired. In jumping, broke my leg. I passed all his pickets, rode sixty miles that night with the bone of my leg tearing the flesh at every jump. I can never repent it, though we hated to kill. Our country owed all her troubles to him, and God simply made me the instrument of his punishment. The country is not . . . what it was. This forced Union is not what I have loved. I care not what becomes of me. I have no desire to outlive my country. This night, before the deed, I wrote a longer article and left it for one of the editors of the National Intelligencer, *in which I fully set forth our reasons for our proceeding.*

---

*Latin for "Thus Always to Tyrants," the Virginia state motto, adopted in 1776.

❊ ❊ ❊

A DREAM DEFERRED

You may be disappointed if you fail, but you are doomed if you don't try.

—Beverly Sills

There is a question posed to us all. It presents itself early on, yet it takes some of us a lifetime to answer—if we answer it at all. What do you want to be when you grow up? It's so much fun to answer initially—when the sky is the lowest limit. When every option is cool: fireman, postman, doctor, trucker, pilot, movie star, teacher, nurse, dancer, ice-skater. When your imagination is fully fueled, and all you have to do to make it happen is to say it aloud and put on a funny hat. For some, it is that easy—they are lucky to encounter their destiny early on and follow it forward. My friend's brother received a magic set for Christmas when he was five and now he's an accomplished illusionist (*michaelgrandinetti.com*). For others, there's a bit more internal wrangling involved. My roommate in college entered as a business major and exited on her way to being a music teacher. She was a rare one who managed to figure it out before she left school: Many can't know what they want from a career until they experience the career itself. The combinations, possibilities, and probabilities involved in finding what you love—or don't love or are just okay with or don't love but like the large salary or just view as a means to an end—are infinite. What nobody tells you while you're prancing around the house with a "hose" in hand, asking Mommy where the fire is, is how much wear and tear your career choice will have on you as a person. At times, it will exhaust you physically, but if you don't find meaning in your work, then it is guaranteed to exhaust you spiritually as well. The only person allowed to decide what completes you is you.

It'll come as no surprise that I suggest answering these questions of vocation in your journal. Write about what gives you pleasure (tennis, photography) and what gives you displeasure (dealing in numbers, working with children). You'll notice patterns and recurring ideas. You'll give birth to ideas both large and small. You'll help yourself through the disappointing periods, and you can certainly congratulate yourself when it's called for. It may take some wading around, but you'll find those things that give you delight and fulfillment, and if you can single those things out and transform them into a paying gig, then you've done yourself and your loved ones a great service. Even if you can't turn your hobby into a working factory, indulging in an activity, sport, or craft on the side will work wonders on your mental well-being.

My journal has been the GPS on my road trip to becoming a writer. You may think that makes too much sense—I am a writer and therefore writing in a journal would help me more than it would help most. Yes and no. Even standing underneath the pink parasol of a writing career, I find the choices are unlimited: books, magazines, newspapers, fiction, nonfiction, historical fiction, prescriptive, objective, subjective, epistolary, narrative. I could go on and on. Writers, like everybody else, must identify their strengths and weaknesses and so they, too, are required to play several rounds of trial and error. Also, writing professionally, as you can imagine, is very different from keeping a journal. I've run to my journal on countless occasions just to have a place (just one place) where no editor could divide and conquer with her red pen. And I still needed to step outside my day job, even though it was a writing day job, to accomplish my deep-seated desires.

By the time I was twenty-three, I had been fired once and laid off once. I am so glad these letdowns took place early in my career—they equipped me for all the uncertainties that come with the working world. I also learned a lesson, with regard to being fired, about stepping outside my assigned boundaries. In both disappointing cases, I ran straight to my journal to steady myself and come up with a contingency plan. By the time I was told I was being laid off for the second time, at the age of twenty-seven, I was sitting in the HR office biting my cheeks together to keep from smiling. The universe was sending me on an indefinite vacation.

Now please don't think my time in magazines was all bad. I had mostly pleasant experiences—wonderful people, engaging work—but the problem was, I never wrote the way I wanted. And that's how it goes when you write for a magazine: You need to make your voice mimic that of the publication. In doing this, I learned a great deal about self-regulation and deadlines, but in order to give my voice some airtime, I worked on two outside projects. One was the novel I spoke of and offered a sample of earlier (page 79). The other self-assigned project was the Web site I mentioned (page 36). It was billed as an online letter-writing service, which it was, but more than that, it was a place to call my own. A place where I could write the way I wanted and no red pen could stop me. Of course, no one was obliged to visit the site either, but the sweet sliver of freedom made it worth it. Before that year was over (2005), a publisher spotted the site and asked if I'd be interested in writing a guide to letter writing. Again, not right away and not without some hard work on my part and wheeling and dealing on my agent's part, the transaction went forth and I wrote my first book—the way I wanted. The moral of the story is: See your absurd ideas through. Follow your gut as far as it's willing to take you.

I've compiled some journal entries that coincide with my trip down the vocational Yellow Brick Road. I haven't arrived at the Emerald City yet, and I hope I never do. I hope to always see it in the distance and keep working toward it, and delight in new challenges all along the way. I'll have you know one other thing aside from being true to yourself: Failure and setbacks are as important in any career as success. With failure comes the knowledge of how to avoid failure in the future. You'll discover what your limits are and how to pull yourself back up. Remember: There is always (always!) more to learn and do. After twenty-seven years working for the same institution, my father obtained his bachelor's degree at the age of fifty-four. After serving in the army and then having a long-standing career with IBM, my grandfather earned his bachelor's at the age of sixty-three. If that's not ambition, I don't know what is.

AT TWENTY-ONE

January 27, 2001
If I had to describe what I do at the magazine* it would be this . . . I fall in love with words and I am forced to abandon them all. I am about to rewrite an article for the third time and I'm terrified. Terrified that it'll be hated all over again and I'll be forced to call myself into question. I'm determined to show them (i.e., my editor, my boyfriend, anyone else who'll read) that I am a good goddamn writer. But what if I start trekking and I realize that I'm really not . . . at all.

August 14, 2001
It's in me now. The desperate desire to be a writer. It feels proud and good. Although, now that I'm at *O* magazine I'm realizing how difficult

* *Pittsburgh* magazine

it will be to be a writer. The time is demanding. Hopefully a character will be built. I'm not sure if a women's magazine is where I want to stay. Don't get me wrong, I love women but I have no edge. I need an edge.

August 29, 2001

[We'll call this a case of blind ambition. . . .]

Fired! Yes, for the first time in my life. Not a great way to begin a career. I went behind the back of P——, the marketing director, and tried to obtain tickets to a runway show. I knew I was being sneaky but didn't think I was doing something harmful. Apparently, I was. P—— was not pleased when she found my fax. I apologized profusely and tried to explain that my intentions were only to see a runway show. Telling T—— and B—— was an expected nightmare. T—— turned into an ice sculpture before my eyes and nodded her head with no inclination of accepting my apology. B——, who I told over the phone, refused to recognize that what I did was a mistake and not an intentionally evil deed. She grew angrier over the phone and barely said good-bye to me.

C—— accepted my apology but approved my dismissal, which I understand. N—— offered kindness and apathy as he always has in the past. H——, surprisingly enough, gave me the most warmth of all and said, "You're allowed to make mistakes." K—— also gave me great comfort. She was a saint and provided me with the kindness of a mother. I know I've earned this punishment and it's a difficult lesson to learn but one I am most grateful for. I have swallowed hard and now it's time to keep moving.

Everything worth doing starts with being scared.

—Art Garfunkel, copied into my journal on December 21, 2003

AT TWENTY-THREE

1/5/2003

I just wrote the first 220 words of my book. Feels frightening, feels amazing. It wouldn't feel that frightening if I hadn't just been rejected by Maxim. But I was so now I'm questioning my ability to do this. My abilities don't matter that much — I mean of course they do, but I know if I don't do this it'll eat me alive. I can't have that.

AT TWENTY-FOUR

October 15, 2003

I lost it yesterday. Gone. My optimism decided I was no longer worth the effort. I had an interview at *Town and Country.* As soon as it ended I quickly decided there's no way I can get the job and so I lost it. Tears streamed all the way down Madison Avenue. The stress of being out of work for months and realizing that a positive attitude isn't ever really going to get me a job caught up with me. And the tears felt good . . . feeling sorry for myself felt so good. I didn't want it to but it did. And now I don't know what to do . . . keep trying . . . obviously. But what happens when trying doesn't do me any good? What happens if and when I have to leave my lovely city? . . . I'm being dramatic. I know.

There is a shabby nobility in failing all by yourself.

—One of many quotes copied into my journal from
   Jay McInerney's *Bright Lights, Big City,* in May 2004

AT TWENTY-SEVEN

[The book I've been talking about up to this point was a self-assigned novel. The book to which I refer after December 2005 is nonfiction and my first published book, *For the Love of Letters.*]

October 3, 2006

Nothing went wrong. Nothing. I got a book deal. Wrote a book. Turned it in. Spent a month editing it, and it's out of my hands for a while.

What a gift this has been! I hope to keep the momentum going and put together a great publicity campaign.

EXPRESS YOURSELF
WITH GOALS AND LISTS

It sounds simple and obvious, but it works. Writing down your goals makes them seem more official and concrete. They become a force to be reckoned with and not something that can be set aside easily. A journal is a great place not only to keep a tally of your goals but also to first figure out exactly what your goals are—that can be more difficult than accomplishing them sometimes.

- **Set Literal Goals:** I was chatting with one of my neighbors a few years back and I asked him what his New Year's resolution was. He said, "I resolve not to make resolutions only at New Year's." That was an excellent idea, I thought, so I stole it right away. I think we should set our aspirations on ROTATE. Have them in constant motion. The goals can be any size or shape—sometimes it takes the little ones, like "Clean out my office," to pave the way for the big ones, like "Start writing my dissertation"—and granting yourself permission to set goals at any time and in any place means they are made and, ideally, met on a more regular basis. I set myself some monthly goals one March: "March 2, 2003—I'm making the most of March. I've decided. I'll send in my FOB* idea this week, I'll finish my first chapter, I'll send away for my tax refund, I'll find a new obsession. It's gonna be a great month. I've decided."

*FOB is magazine lingo for "front of book." I was pitching a short article to some magazine.

- **Set Abstract Goals:** You are a work in progress and should keep an eye out for ways to better yourself. Keeping track of the personality improvements you'd like to make and the improvements you've made is a good way to align the person you want to be with the person you are. As always, leave room to fall short of perfection. Here's one of my lists of abstract objectives: "May 11, 2002—I found her today: The woman I want to be. She's kind, polite, and reasonable, but not a pushover. Her assertiveness is a form of self-defense revealed when people are trying to take advantage of her. She's insightful and intelligent. She's not afraid to admit when she doesn't understand something. She's a constructive critic. She's valuable. She's brave. She's sexual. She admires women. She adores men. She fears and reveres God. She's compassionate. She's charitable. She's open. She's flawed. She finds pleasure in simple things and finds beauty in all things. Now that I found her I do hope I can become her."

- **Set Short-Term Goals:** Short-term goals can be as simple as "I'm going to mow the lawn today" or "I'm taking that bag of stuff to Goodwill." The reason to set short-term goals is to get in the habit of writing what you're going to do and then doing it. There's a small sense of accomplishment in every dusty corner—promise yourself you'll sweep it out, and once you do, you'll know what I'm talking about.

- **Set Long-Term Goals:** Once you've gotten yourself in the wonderful habit of *writing/doing/writing/doing* the smaller things, it'll hopefully translate to the bigger things. Super-sized goals are usually just a combination of many little goals. For example, the family vacation to Europe you've been meaning to take requires the blending of saving enough money, working for six more months so you earn an extra week of vacation, and (the fun part) sitting down and planning the trip.

Ask Yourself

— If I could do anything (*anything!*), what would it be? For example: My sister said the other day, "I wish someone would pay me to interpret song lyrics." Now take your idea and see if it translates into a Web site, a blog, a short story, a script, a class you can take, a small business you can start, or an already existing occupation you can pursue.

— What did I want to be in high school/college?

— Why didn't I pursue that?

— If you are exactly where you want to be professionally, ask yourself what improvements can be made. What's the next best challenge?

Tell Yourself

— When you've done something you're proud of.

— When you've done something you're not proud of (but offer suggestions on how you can improve the situation if it were to arise again).

— What you'd like to accomplish this year/month/week/day.

— What you wish you would have accomplished a while back, then try to create an updated version of the goal.

— What your favorite work related qualities about yourself are.

ALTERNATE AMBITION

As I mentioned earlier, I think failure is as important as success in life but especially in career pursuits. Failure forces you to face yourself, ask what went wrong, and wonder what improvements can be made. It'll either break you or make you that much more determined to prove to the person who fired you or didn't hire you, or simply to yourself, that you can accomplish that which you set your mind to. It might also serve to suggest that you just weren't meant to do the thing you failed at. Admitting that isn't giving up, it's taking knowledge and experience and applying it elsewhere.

I suppose I can't keep it from you any longer: Once upon a time, I *really* wanted to be a model. I had no good reason for wanting it. Basically, I wanted to be famous and I really didn't care what form that took. I'd feel ridiculous coming clean about that except I think most of us have the vision of fame for ourselves at some point. We want it because, from a distance, it appears to be a life both glamorous and easy, and because it also seems, for some curious reason, like a life we deserve. The pursuit alone practically says, *Well, of course, people should be interested in me!* I won't say this is bad, because it takes a soupçon of ego to do just about anything. You'll never try out for the cheerleading squad, stand on a soapbox, sit in the director's chair, or show off your premier polka skills if you don't believe yourself to be intelligent, talented, or simply capable of such things. A sense of self-importance and awareness of one's ability is good. What keeps these traits from becoming insufferable conceit is willingness to accept humility at face value, a working knowledge of all the things you can't do, and great admiration for those who can.

I never pursued acting with brazen force, but to my mild embarrassment these days, I did pursue modeling. I was nineteen and impetuous. After the spring semester of my sophomore year, I moved to Connecticut to live with my aunt, and from there I ventured into New York City almost daily to meet with agencies and eventually clients. At the start of the summer, I was certain everything would tilt instantly toward my dreams and I wouldn't have to return to school in the fall. I started working with an agency called Click right away, which was a good sign, but none of their clients hired me, which was a very bad sign. By the end of the summer, I had conceded, and instead of yearning for fortune and fame, all I wanted was to be hired for at least one job, but it never happened.

The overall experience was invaluable, but you couldn't convince me of that at the time. I felt frustrated and defeated. I was doing everything I was told and didn't understand why it still wasn't coming together. I turned to my journal often that summer—sometimes to lash out and other times to assuage my frustration. I whispered to myself on those pages the same way one gently repeats to a sniffling child, "You're okay. It'll be all right." I also talked myself out of giving up several times; it didn't make me a supermodel (or even a catalog model), but I mastered the art of not giving up in other areas of my life. Ultimately, I learned that modeling wasn't for me or rather that I wasn't for modeling. I've since shared many an elevator with young girls on magazine go-sees (the industry term for casting calls), and there's an angular, edgy look to them that I do not possess. If people tell me now that I should model, I do say thank you—it's a great compliment—but I think to myself, *No, really, I shouldn't.* And I'm glad I know that for sure.

June 24, 1999

I'm here. Trying not to think about New York, but it's not working. New York was disappointing. I appeared at an IGM open call today. The office was intimidating. The staff was efficient and cold. They didn't look at any of the girls in the flesh. They took our portfolios and handed them back to us with icy little notes proclaiming their disinterest. I wasn't offended. I mentally prepared myself to arrive punctually for my L'Oréal go-see.

June 29, 1999

Clear! He yells "Clear!" in my ear with his obnoxious Brooklyn accent and heartless attitude. The rapport between us is diminishing. His faith is fading, and unfortunately so is mine. Now what? At what point is it appropriate to give up? Clear . . . meaning there's nothing on my schedule. I'm being battered and bruised by the modeling industry . . . but I haven't been completely pushed over yet.

July 1, 1999

The enemy has arrived. I haven't tried on clothes in months. The money I make babysitting ensures me transportation directly to the sublime platforms of Grand Central Station. I'm in New York with a long face and weary body. I have been successfully rejected by 5 prestigious modeling agencies and by 5 clients associated with Click. My patience is paper thin, and I don't know where to jump from here. I'd give almost anything to know the outcome of my story. I am, however, feeling a little successful. After 10 rejections I'm only starting to feel it. I'm more resilient than I've ever been before. I have enjoyed seeing each agency. I am surprised though. Modeling agencies make so much money. I expected their lobbies to be grand and impressive, but I was very wrong.

June 2000

[I was back in New York—not necessarily for modeling this time. But I was approached by a photographer and ended up shooting with him. *Test* in the world of photography simply means "take pictures."]

I don't know when I became a woman, nor do I know when I became a woman willing to pose naked for an anxious camera. It was an average morning when Hanz, a 5th Avenue photographer, approached me. "Do you test?" he asked. "With those eyes you have to be a model." Before I could blush too much he handed me his card. The picture on it was majestic and sexy. . . .

At the shoot I just removed my clothes. I didn't put a great deal of thought into whether it was right or wrong. All I knew was that I felt natural and comfortable. I didn't feel immodest or dirty. I felt pure.

ON BEING NAKED
IN FRONT OF STRANGERS

Well, I suppose I can't mention posing naked and not explain myself further. I get such an uneasy kick out of that last entry because it's so seemingly mindless: "At the shoot I just removed my clothes. I didn't put a great deal of thought into whether it was right or wrong." I'm perplexed—why did I choose not to write that the photographer wasn't after cheap thrills, but was instead very professional throughout the entire day? And that I had seen many of his other nudes before deciding to become one of them? Or that the photos were shot in black and white—lending themselves instantly to art rather than pornography?

Perhaps the reason I didn't go into greater detail about the experience was that I tend to lean on my memory to fill in the blanks of my journal sometimes. An entry such as the posing naked one, which is written quickly and carelessly, serves to remind me of the incident. Once I reread something like that, I usually have an *Oh, yeah. I remember that* thought and all the details surrounding the day come soaring back. What the quick and careless entry served to do was frame the emotions of the moment. This is important because feelings in retrospect can be quite different than they were at the time the episode took place. I could recount that entire photo shoot for you, but it would lack the whimsy I unthinkingly inserted into the story when I was nineteen.

Don't get me wrong. I'm all about retrospection. I think it's a great gift to be able to look back and see something you didn't see before, but I also like being able to access the sensations belonging only to that one moment—even if they are naive and foolish, there is charm in that. For those of you with fleeting memories, you might be careful to include more precise details in your journal entries, as they may serve as your memory someday.

SINS OF THE MOTHER

Oftentimes, in addition to career pursuits, we look to starting a family for that which will fulfill us internally and give our lives renewed purpose. Getting married and having children are singled out as two of life's most important, extraordinary, and soul-satisfying acts. As a consummate observer of my fellow human beings, I've noticed that because the expectation bar on these two events is set so high, the letdown levels can be pretty low. This isn't to say husbands, wives, mothers, and fathers don't learn to roll with the punches, but sometimes they don't anticipate them and suffer out of sheer surprise and faulty preparation. Then again, maybe the growing pains of harvesting a home are just that, and the degree of difficulty is not something one could ever anticipate.

Here is the journal entry of a woman dealing with the unexpectedly draining aspects of her present occupation: motherhood. The mother is my very own, and the child screaming at the top of her lungs is the much shorter yet equally stubborn two-year-old me. Here, my mother walks the tightrope between her career and her children. She longs to be a good mother while still wanting to see her ambitions through. She's exhausted, fed up, and wanting to quit a job she can't quit.

I was struck by the raw, endearing honesty of this write-up. She clearly felt no need to convince herself she felt magical about motherhood just because that's what was expected. She was honest with herself when she wrote this, and she went on to be notably honest with my sister and me about such things. I broke up with a boyfriend in high school and she asked why. I said because I just didn't feel the same way about him any-more. She replied matter-of-factly, "Just so you know, you're not always going to feel the same way about your husband." She never pretended be-ing married or having children was easy, but always made sure we knew it was worth it.

The following entry was written circa April 1982. It wasn't dated, but I'm surmising based on the ages of my sister and myself. This wasn't found in a journal, though my mother has countless volumes of them, but rather typed on a stray sheet of white paper. My mom found it and could hardly read it aloud because she was laughing so hard. She was not, I'll venture to guess, laughing when she wrote it. For the record, my mother is a good mother. She's an excellent mother, and I find it a com-fort to know that even very good mothers can have a very bad time of motherhood.

I am an intelligent woman. I have two beautiful children. At the moment they are both driving me up the wall. The older one is lying in her bed—which has come unhinged because of her jumping on it—and she is screaming at the top of her lungs. She has become overtired, in my opinion; her gums are hurting her because she is cutting her two-year molars (a little late, she's 2½) and she is venting with all the gup she can muster. I have been as patient as I can muster. I have gone up to her several times. I have given her baby aspirin substitute. I have brought her water. I have blown her nose. I have tried to comfort her. And finally I have threatened, "If you don't stop crying, Samara, I will keep your door shut. I don't want to hear you anymore."

There is a very grave fear here. It is that I will not be able to overcome the obstacles that my mother faced. I don't want to be a secretary all my working life; I don't want to be a manuscript typist. I want to research the books myself. I want to write the articles, and I want to teach the classes. I want to fly in an airplane, share knowledge with others, and I want to raise my children.

Earlier in the day I found myself crying in frustration in my kitchen. Some of my words were, "I am tired of being thrown up on and tired of cleaning up shit and tired of trying to change my intellect into something a two-year-old will understand." SHE IS STILL CRYING *** SHE REFUSES TO QUIT ** I HAVE TO BLARE MOZART TO DROWN THE SOUND OF HER SOBS ** MY 4 MONTH OLD WILL BE AWAKENED BY THE SOUND ** I QUIT I QUIT I QUIT ** THIS JOB SUCKS

LOUISA MAY ALCOTT (1832–1888) ON GIVING BIRTH TO YOUR FIRST BOOK

Louisa May Alcott, best known for her book *Little Women*, was born in Germantown, Pennsylvania, (now part of Philadelphia), but was raised in Concord, Massachusetts, as her parents moved there when she was two years old. She grew up surrounded by transcendental philosophy and New England liberalism—her parents were friends with both Ralph Waldo Emerson and Henry David Thoreau and were also steadfast supporters of abolition and the emerging women's suffrage movement. Louisa's father, Bronson Alcott, preferred hosting philosophy seminars to earning a living for his family, so Louisa caught on early that she would

Louisa May Alcott at Age Twenty

have to be monetarily responsible. She held many jobs, including teaching, sewing, and acting as a nanny to families in Boston.

Louisa was a lifelong journaler. She began writing at the age of eleven and wrote up to March 1888, the month of her death at the age of fifty-five. Her first published work was a poem entitled "Sunlight," which was printed in *Peterson's Magazine.* Her first book, *Flower Fables,* a collection of stories she once wrote for Emerson's daughter, Ellen, was published when she was twenty-two. In a letter she wrote to her mother on Christmas Day, 1854, Louisa says, "Into your Christmas stocking I have put my 'first-born,' knowing you will accept it with all its faults (for grandmothers are always kind)." She lovingly refers to *Flower Fables* as her firstborn in her journal as well. At the time, writing was just another means of making money for Louisa. In October 1868, at the age of thirty-five, she published the first part of *Little Women.* By the age of forty, she had gotten her family completely out of debt. Louisa wrote professionally until she died of mercury poisoning, as a result of treatment for typhoid which she had contracted while working as a nurse during the Civil War. She published twenty books in her lifetime.

PINCKNEY STREET, BOSTON, Jan. 1, 1855—The principal event of the winter is the appearance of my first book "Flower Fables." An edition of sixteen hundred. It has sold very well, and people seem to like it. I feel quite proud that the little tales I wrote for Ellen E. when I was sixteen should now bring money and fame.

I will put some of the notices in "varieties." Mothers are always foolish over their first-born.

Miss Wealthy Stevens paid for the book, and I received $32.

April 1855—I am in the garret with my papers round me and a pile of apples to eat while I write my journal, plan stories, and enjoy the patter of rain on the roof.

Being behindhand, as usual, I'll make note of the main events up to date, for I don't waste ink in the poetry pages of rubbish now. I've begun to live, and have no time for sentimental musing.

In October I began my school, Father talked, Mother looked after her boarders, and tried to help everybody. Anna was in Syracuse teaching Mrs. S's children.

My book came out, and people began to think that topsey-turvy Louisa would amount to something after all, since she could do so well as housemaid, teacher, seamstress, and story-teller. Perhaps she may.

In February I wrote a story for which C. paid $5, and asked for more.

In March I wrote a farce for W. Warren, and Dr. W. offered it to him, but W.W. was too busy.

Also began another tale, but found little time to work on it, with school, sewing, and house-work. My winter's earnings are—

> *School, one quarter $50*
> *Sewing $50*
> *Stories $20*

if I am ever paid.

A busy and a pleasant writer, because, though hard at times, I do seem to be getting on a little, and that encourages me.

Have heard Lowell and Hedge lecture, acted in plays, and thanks to our rag money and good cousin H., have been to the theater several times,—always my great joy.

Summer plans are yet unsettled. Father wants to go to England: not a wise idea I think. We shall probably stay here, and A and I go into the country as governesses. It's a queer way to live, but dramatic, and I rather like it, for we never know what is to come next. We are real "Micawbers," and always "ready for spring."

I have planned a Christmas book and hope to be able to write it.

CHAPTER 11

✳ ✳ ✳

INTIMATE DETAILS

She'd been neither a saint nor a whore, but a fallible, sexual woman.

—Wally Lamb

(One of the many quotes copied into my journal in May 2003 from Wally Lamb's
bestseller *She's Come Undone*)

I imagine many of you skipped right to this chapter. Hey, it's the first place I'd go, too. When we go through someone else's journal, this is usually the type of private writing we hope to find, and in doing so we are searching for ourselves. We are looking to see if the journal writer has any of the same sexual insecurities or frustrations that we do. Or we are looking to see how sex plays out on someone else's page so as to compare it to our own. If we lack experience, then we might be curious to witness how it works. We may simply be looking for ideas, or to get turned on. I can only hope I don't disappoint.

Sex is unique in that it is both very private and very public. Ads, music videos, magazines, and pornography sensationalize sex. These media tell us what our sex lives are supposed to be like, and we feel most inadequate if they aren't up to snuff. Coming from the other megaphone is the religious right saying we shouldn't be concerned with sex until we're fastened into our matrimonial seats. It's a wonder we ever find our sexual selves at all. Andy Warhol once said, "Sex is the biggest nothing of all time." The first time I read that, I thought, *Yes! Exactly!* When I tried to relay it to a friend, she said, "What the hell does that mean?" Who knows what it actually means—this is Andy Warhol we're talking about—but my instant, enthusiastic interpretation was that it's this nothing we fall for again and again. We're either up in arms about it or we're panting at the promise of it, and it's not that big of a deal.

I shouldn't say it's not a big deal. It is a very big deal in the context of each of our lives, and it's worth silencing the rest of the world to figure out what our sexual intrigues, fantasies, beliefs, and apprehensions are. Part of the problem with our sex-drenched society is just that—you're told you should want it at all times, and maybe you really don't. Or perhaps you've become obsessed with sex as an ideal and can't enjoy it on a raw, human level. 'Tis true that sex isn't always sexy. What seems so obvious—your likes and dislikes—can benefit from further self-exploration. A journal offers a safe place, provided you hide it well, to open up about your sexual desires and demons.

Although I have thought about sex in explicit detail for what seems like the majority of my life, or at least from ten and up, I didn't start having it until I was in college. Until I was eighteen, I believed, and wasn't ashamed to admit, that I wouldn't have sex until I was married. When I was eighteen, I changed my mind. I didn't change it for any splendid reason. I was decidedly and understandably curious. I also realized, at some point, that waiting until I was married to have sex was never my idea—it was what I was told I should do. It all worked out for the best. I'm glad I waited until I was out of high school to have sex, and I'm also glad I didn't wait until I was married. The part I wasn't so glad about was losing my virginity itself—a semi-traumatic experience, but I think it's that way for many people. You can't be told to do this thing (by all your friends) and not to do this thing (by all authority) and not be let down by it in some way initially. Thankfully, sex gets better over time. The more comfortable you become with yourself the more comfortable you become with it. And it's worth the investment to experiment and explore, to spend many creative hours on this important (yes, I said it) aspect of your being.

In the selection of journal entries here, I did not include the one about losing my virginity, but only because I never wrote about it. What I have included are some of the awkward, treacherous, emotional, wonderful, intimate details on the road to sexual salvation. My story begins at sixteen—because like all teenagers who promise to wait to have sex, I, too, was tempted by the "everything but" clause. Your story may be very different from mine. Perhaps you started having sex much earlier or much later. Wherever you are in your sexuality—having it five times a day, having not had it in years, waiting to get the spark back, wanting to meet the right person, chronically masturbating—don't be afraid to write about it. Buy a lockbox or burn the pages if you must, but face your sexual self until you feel healthy and satisfied.

AT SIXTEEN

May 17, 1996

I always get embarrassed writing about sexual experiences, but for some reason that eludes me and I do it anyway. I suppose I do it because it's a part of my life.

Yesterday Jonathan and I were in his room, with the door open, and we knew we couldn't satisfy our passions with his sick mother across the hall, so we made our way to the basement. We had to be slick and sneak past Gram, but that wasn't a problem.

We found our way into the chilly, damp half-lit basement. There's not much furniture down there so we placed our bodies on a couchlike structure made with pieces of old chairs that he and I put together last time we ventured to the basement.

Our position was comfortable as he began teasing me. His hands wandered everywhere except my pleasure center. His mouth covered my stomach. After all this he shifted so he could pleasure my loins. It worked too, as it always does. He would take whatever liquid came out of me and spread it everywhere down there. Then his hand brought me to climax. After this I knew what I had to do, I moved positions and unzipped him. In a great effort to try and pleasure him he kept indicating (with his hand) exactly what he needed me to do, but I felt like I wasn't strong enough. He then said to me, "You can be more aggressive." At this point I was flustered. I realized I couldn't give him what he needed. The only thing I could think to relieve myself of the frustration and embarrassment was to go down. I needed to make him feel as good as he made me feel. So once again I switched positions. Little did I know how nervous I was going to get. I was on top of him and I started shaking. I felt sick, but I was ready and willing to force myself down. He caught on and pulled himself up. I said, "I'm sorry," and he asked for what. I said, "I was going to fix it." He told me he wouldn't let me . . . so after this we had a conversation about orgasms. He told me I was the best he ever had. He only says that because he's understanding, patient, and sweet, not because I give him any pleasure. So I decided this fooling around thing has to stop, at least for a little while, because I can't take it if I can't give it.

AT EIGHTEEN

January 19, 1998
Bill and I reached a new level in our sexual relationship. Am I still a virgin? Barely! He tied me up then proceeded to turn the lights on

(which he knows I hate). I used the word *fuck* a numerous amount of times. So at one point something along the lines of do you want to fuck me came propelling from my mouth. I didn't think he would because there was no protection, but he opened me up and began to enter. I jolted and said No! I'm sure that didn't make him happy, but it would have done more harm than good. The weekend overall was pretty good. I mean as good as it gets for Bill and I. The arguments were minimal and none of them serious.

AT NINETEEN

February 16, 1999

I want to conquer sex. I want it to be the pleasure, control, and confection that allows me to be a woman. I want it to fortify me. I am tired of subscribing to it. I am tired of it deciding my insecurities and aggravations. I look and see faces that have been beneath me in salacious intercourse. I see them fully clothed and laughing about, but I can blink and bring myself back to the bed where we sinned in constant motion.

AT TWENTY-FOUR

February 14, 2004

It's 11:45—15 more minutes of Valentine's Day left, and I just came to tell you what a wonderful day I've had. It started last night—Stan took me to a movie premiere (*Spontaneous Combustion*)*—he was in it for about 5 minutes. Then we went to the after party at the Gershwin Hotel. The lighting was red and the crowd was fun. We went back to

* Not the movie's actual title.

Stan's around 2:30 a.m.—we had sex and blew lines until 4:30. I had written him a letter the day before explaining that I liked him but was still suffering another. He understood and appreciated the letter—so I felt like we were on the same page all night. We both slept a severe sleep and woke up/had sex/and slept until 3:10 p.m. When we woke he recited a sonnet for me and I recited my 5th grade tree poem for him. I enjoyed his company and relaxed in his presence. I returned to the city just in time to have dinner with Elise and her father. Her brother Tao also came. We ate a splendid meal at Rosa Mexicano uptown.

AT TWENTY-SIX

July 28, 2006

I am naked and alone. Except alone is no longer a bad thing and naked is a wonderful thing so this is to say I am very happy at the moment. I took the day off and went to the library—I finished writing my Letters to the Editor chapter and the Introduction, which have been difficult for me. I ran two miles at sunset with a glorious breeze escorting me the entire time, and I just had a savory orgasm. I had one this morning and thought another would take too long, but my body was begging me. I stripped down and put my vibrator directly on my clit. It was an intense and borderline painful sensation until I could feel myself about to come. I'm exhausted now and will sleep well I can tell.

EXPRESS YOURSELF EXPLICITLY

Knowing yourself sexually isn't as simple as knowing what your pleasure points are. It's important also to take note of your emotional expectations and reactions and to be aware of your sexuality when you're not having sex. It is with us at all times. Writing about sex is undeniably awkward at first, but so is having sex. You'll get used to it and will hopefully come to enjoy the process. If the sex is good, I very much enjoy having it twice—in person and on paper. And if it's lackluster, then writing can be an important tool in figuring out exactly what went wrong and how it can be improved upon.

- **A Sexual Stream of Consciousness:** Open the floodgates. Do not think, just write. Write about the pleasures, pains, frustrations, fears, delights, shortcomings, and satisfactions of your sex life. Start with whoever or whatever comes immediately to mind when you hear the word *sex* and go from there. If you've never written about sex before, this is probably the best technique to get started with. As with any stream-of-consciousness writing, you will shock yourself.

- **Past and Present:** Much of the way we experience sex now has to do with the way we were first introduced to it. Even if your early sexual experiences aren't something you think about on a daily basis anymore, they can still be affecting your current sex life. Consider reliving your first sexual encounters through your journal. You will visit the past with more knowledge about the practice and also about people. If your partner made you feel insecure at the time, perhaps you can see now that it was, in fact, his or her own insecurities being projected onto you.

- **The Couple's Diary:** For as close as you have to be with another human being to have sex, there can be a wide margin of misunderstanding. One of you thinks the sex is fantastic, while the other hasn't been satisfied in months. One party has been fine with everything thus far but is ready to try something a little more risqué. Consider starting a diary where you and your partner are open about your sex life. You can each recount an episode from your different points of view and see what's working and what's not or write your fantasies. Don't be shy; remember, this person has already seen you naked.

WAYS TO GET STARTED WRITING

Ask Yourself

- Am I happy with my sex life now? (This can include masturbating if you don't have a partner at present.) If no, what improvements could be made?

- Am I comfortable talking to my partner about my needs? Why or why not?

- How do I feel about my body in general?

- What were some of the surprises and disappointments of losing my virginity? What were some of my sexual expectations and fears?

Tell Yourself

- The most pleasant sexual experiences you've had and what made them so.

- The most uncomfortable sexual experiences you've had and what made them so.

- Your earliest sexual fantasy.

- Your most recent sexual fantasy.

- Your ideal sexual scenario.

- The first person you had a sexual longing for.

THE VIOLIN CONCERTO; OR, LESSONS IN TAKING A LOVER

I've always wanted to give something two titles. It was once very common for a work of literature to have two titles, and I still find it charming. The full title of Mary Shelley's *Frankenstein* is *Frankenstein; or, The Modern Prometheus* (1818) and Herman Melville's masterpiece is *Moby Dick; or, The Whale* (1851). A comparatively recent two-title toss is James Frey's breakout memoir *A Million Little Pieces; or, Please Oprah Don't Hurt Me* (2003). Now it's my turn to have some fun playing "two titles are better than one."

That was my way of breaking the ice before we address the fact that you've seen me pretty much naked at this point. Yet even after our saunter down personal sexual history lane, it feels strange to now continue the story and admit this next fact: After dating the dapper gentleman who I wrote about on Valentine's Day, 2004, I didn't have sex for almost two years. My journal didn't have sex for almost three. These things happen. I do advocate periods of abstinence if an emotional regroup is in order, as it was in my case. I consciously said to myself that I wouldn't have sex for a while. I did not plan on it being that long.

What cast my dry spell was a chemical explosion. What caused my journal's bout was my chemical explosion followed by two uninspiring lovers. The explosion first: I was dating a man who I adored, and I wanted more than anything to be in a relationship with him. All signs pointed to us heading in that direction, and then it ended suddenly and without my consent. In a perplexing instant, I found myself dating a man who, by no fault of his own, I did not adore. His many redeeming qualities were swept away in the mighty current of my feelings for the first man. I continued to date him because I felt as though I wasn't trying to move on if I didn't. That wasn't fair to anyone. Throughout my body, the positive sexual charge of the first man resisted the negative sexual charge of the second, and I suffered severe internal injuries.

I made a semi-solemn vow that I would not have sex again unless it was with someone I was excited about—as in I can't sleep, as in my journal is sick of me gushing about this guy, as in Céline Dion sounds really good right now. That's one of those things if you declare out loud, you set yourself back at least six months, and I did. I ended up on a few dates here and there. They didn't amount to anything. Around month number six of not only no sex but also no inspiring prospects, I tried to bargain with the universe. "Can I have a crush?" I politely requested. "That's all I'm asking for, just someone to focus my energy on and fantasize about." The universe did not see fit to oblige in any way.

As the year (2004) came to an end, I caught a rerun of *The Tonight Show*, and Jay Leno was interviewing Angelina Jolie. She was telling him how she hadn't had sex in a year. Of all the points to identify with her on, I never thought this would be one of them. She continued to talk about how she alleviated this problem by "taking a lover." I love that expression, and I hadn't heard it in a while. The word *lover* alone is stimulating and seductive. Somehow it manages to suggest more than simple, careless sex, without being a full-on commitment. It invites you to squeeze the juice out of the orange and throw the relationship rind away.

I've always had a strange affiliation with the notion of a lover—never knowing exactly what a lover was, but knowing that I wanted to experience one. In some cases, it just literally means the person you're sleeping with, but I also suspected there was more to it than that. On August 18, 2002, I wrote a short journal entry: "I was just strolling through Barnes and Noble looking for a lover. I'm not quite sure why I'm always looking for a lover, but I am. One sordid, passionate lover to indulge me in all things."

When I think of taking a lover, the cliché fantasy of climbing up someone's fire escape wearing nothing but black stilettos and a baby blue raincoat rushes to mind. Angelina maintained that she didn't have feelings for her lover, and Jay insisted that one person always feels for the other. In those tabloid-barren days after Billy Bob but before Brad, Miss Jolie re-romanticized the ideal—at least for me.

Mercy in the Morning

Several times throughout 2005, the universe fulfilled my request. Unfortunately, she interpreted my appeal literally, and I was granted a crush and nothing else. In January 2006, I was inching dangerously close to the two-year mark; my poor journal was getting ready to pull her pages out, too. I decided to forgo the crush and attempt a lover. The gentleman's name was Kyle. He had been a friend by association of mine for three years. He was one of the few men who I had always found physically attractive but wasn't drawn to in any other way. The arrangement was made one evening when I asked our mutual friend, Larry, "Do you think Kyle would be my lover?" Except, in a very un-Jolie way, I believe I used the term *fuck-buddy*.

A few weeks later, Kyle and I found ourselves out and about, figuratively toasting in the name of foreplay. I had met him at his apartment and wasn't exactly sure how the buddy system was supposed to work. He suggested we grab a drink. He was very good at pretending he was none the wiser. Afterward, we returned to his place and fulfilled our unspoken yet well-known purpose. The sex was good. I say this without hesitation. I am one, however, who tries not to judge sex too much on the first go-round. You're dealing with a new person, new techniques, new fantasies, new ideas, and it tends to take a few tries before you can hope to be in tandem. I went to bed excited to play again in the morning, and even more excited to relay the detailed art of taking a lover to my dear diary.

The morning came and went. Kyle left the room before I awoke, and I found him sitting at the kitchen table. I was hoping that, when he saw I was awake, we'd go back into his room. Since he didn't motion to do that right away, I sat down. We flipped through magazines and made cordial small talk. I continued to naively wonder when we were going to go back into his room. Was I supposed to initiate it? He asked me about my plans for the day and elaborated on his. Kyle's next grand gesture was to get in the shower. I gave up, got dressed, and waited until he was done to say good-bye. When I left, I walked through the long, fluorescent-lit hallway of self-consciousness, thinking, *Wow, he didn't enjoy that at all. He didn't even want to do it again.*

Needless to say, I was taken aback when I heard from Kyle the following week. He wanted to meet, and so we did. The scene played out almost exactly as it had the first time. Drinks. Sex. No morning sex. If you sleep with someone and then don't sleep with them again until a week later, you basically start from scratch—so again, the sex was good, but I didn't feel like any progress was being made. It should have been easy for me to throw my arm around him or something of the sort first thing in the morning to indicate how hungry I was, but he slept at least two human bodies away from me in the standoffish, almost fetal, position. I understand he did this to draw the line between fact and fantasy, which is fine. My concern was *If this is about sex, why aren't we having it?* We got together a few more times. We enjoyed ourselves, but all of my attempts to have sex more than once were thwarted. I ended our lovership shortly thereafter. I did this based on my perpetual self-consciousness that only morning sex could cure.

How My Journal Got Her Groove Back

My journal knows nothing of my attempted lover. That wasn't a conscious decision. It's not as though I folded my arms in protest and refused to write—I was simply uninspired. Shortly after Kyle, I went on a life-altering blind date (page 42). Although that man helped me come to terms with the fact that being single might just be written in my stars, I wasn't nearly as willing to reconcile a life of no sex. Toward the end of 2006, I gave it a go with one more lover (story really not worth telling), and then I did have sex worth writing about (page 91). It was with my love. My darling. My weakness. My muse. My Tyler. He's the one who, at the beginning of the section, pushed me out of his exclusive airplane into this godforsaken social jungle. I saw him around Christmas. We went out to dinner, and I showed him the new house I'd just bought. We christened it. For a notably selfish man, he is a remarkably unselfish lover. He'd gotten himself into the wonderful habit of treating my body as if it were made of Italian silk. He would have had early-morning *and* late-morning sex with me, I'm sure of it, but he couldn't stay. He had to go home to his fiancée.

I know. I know. You don't have to tell me. I know. Doing something like that is on a par with trying to dry your hair while still in the shower or setting off firecrackers in your living room. But I did it. I set off one firecracker, and I emerged from the rubble with a few cuts and bruises. I said to myself, *Well, genius, now you know what it's like to play with pyrotechnics in the house. Don't do it again.* And I didn't. I realized how short I was selling myself by being his mistress when I wanted to be his everything, but I am glad I did it once. Heaven help me, I am.

As 2007 geared up to make her grand entrance, I promised myself no more old flames. Not a one! And no more force-feeding myself new lovers. Okay, good. Glad that's cleared up. Now what? My living situation was on the brink of change. I had purchased a home in Philadelphia but was still living in New York because of my job. I was looking for a good time to quit and move. Then the most wonderful thing happened: I got laid off. Quitting means champagne and cupcakes on your last day. Getting laid off means severance pay and collecting unemployment for up to six months. This was the second time in my life I had been laid off—I knew the drill. I decided to stick around New York for the month of February and say good-bye to as many people in person as I could. I was set to move on Sunday, March 4. The Friday before I moved, I met up with girl-friends to drink and dance the night away. I'm not sure what it was—the fact that it was late, the fact that I was cranky, the fact that I was moving on Sunday—but the universe saw this as an opportune time for me to meet a man.

March 4, 2007

I don't think I said two words to God in church this morning, which is strange considering this is a day of transition. I officially moved today. No more New York. Not as a resident anyway. I was distracted during the service—by ushering, by reading, and by a boy. I met a sweet, sweet boy on Friday night. His name is Jeremy and we met at Tenjune around 2:30 a.m. I had had it with the noise and the crowd but knew I would stay out because Chloé and Karina had gone to the trouble of meeting me. Jeremy came in on the later side of everything and made my night. The club was way too loud to have any sort of introductory conversation, so we went into the hallway and talked for a while.

It was nice to connect with someone in such an overbearing place. When we were back in the club I didn't expect much more to happen—it was loud again and it was almost 4. I thought I'd leave soon. But we continued talking and later we were dancing. Then we started kissing. I don't remember who kissed who—felt like we kissed each other at the same slow and perfect speed. What a wonderful kisser he is. When I told him it was time to go he kissed me good-bye and was kind not to invite me to go home with him. Instead he invited me to a party he was hosting on Saturday night. I hadn't planned to go out but very much wanted to see him again.

The second night was as amazing as the first. Lots of making out and mingling. I left around 2 a.m. because I knew I had to get up and get going with my mother the next morning. Jeremy kissed me good-bye and said, "This was way too short a time." I told him I could come back up the next Friday if he was free. He responded positively, but that might fade in the light of reality. How ill-timed is my move! I'm not kicking myself though—I think the universe only allowed me to meet him because I'm moving. I hope to hear from him but am grateful for the short shot of infatuation if not. Reminds me that I am (in fact) capable of it.

A Journal Milestone

And just like that, you're a schoolgirl in a short skirt all over again. After I left the party, I sent Jeremy a text message saying what a great time I had. I need to emphasize what an aversion I originally had, sometimes still have, to text messaging. Of course, I forgot all about that when he wrote me back. Now, because I'm kind of a loser and I need things to be tangible, for the first time ever, I copied a text message into my journal:

March 5, 2007, 8:17 A.M.
Right back at you, beautiful. I think we'll have to line up another night out as soon as I can lure you back to New York . . . How's today for you? Hope you recovered okay and I'll see you soon ;) Send me your e-mail when you have a second also, cutie . . .

As it turned out I did not go back to New York the following Friday, but we stayed in touch through March and I made plans to return to the city the last weekend of the month. He e-mailed me a few days before I went up:

Wednesday, March 28, 2007, 11:05 A.M.
Are you still planning on coming to town? If so, any set plans? I have a birthday dinner for a friend of mine on Friday night that I was really hoping to take a date to, but only if she's tall, blonde, and beautiful . . .

Charming isn't he? I thought so. My friend Chloé did not. She liked him by himself, as most would. He's approachable and charismatic—a man of the people, especially the women, if you will. But as far as he and I were concerned, Chloé started singing, "Samara, stay away from him," fairly early on. I recognized the danger in allowing myself to be overly flattered, but I refused to adopt the cynicism necessary not to be. If a man I think is beautiful tells me I'm beautiful, then I am going to become a gooey version of myself, and that's just the way it is.

Before I continue, let me say that this story does have a happy ending—but perhaps not the happy ending that you (or I) would instinctively hope for. I've learned that happy endings come in all shapes and sizes—if you don't look closely sometimes, you might even miss them—and they rarely (if ever) resemble parcels packaged by Disney. You'll note in both of the following journal entries that I am waiting to hear from him. His communication practices were faulty. All of his messages were clever and sweet, but sometimes they would take just long enough to come in and I'd wonder if I was going to hear from him at all. He always came through for me, but this did keep me on guard. Anyway, that's not the point right now. The glorious point at this moment in time is that my journal and I had not gotten this much action in far too long.

April 2, 2007

I want to call him. I can't. I won't. But the desire is strong. An animal within me. He knows he has the right-of-way. He understands. He noted several times this past weekend how we see eye-to-eye on so many things and how rare that is. It is rare. Wonderfully rare. Our whole weekend was rare. It started with drinks at Whiskey Park. Looking at him was such a pleasure. His dark eyes. Half smile. Enchanting. Our conversation was easy—motivated by genuine curiosity.

On the walk over to the dinner party our hands brushed each other's and there was this semi-awkward, very cute moment as we went to hold hands. We didn't hold hands for very long, he let go and offered me his old-fashioned arm instead. Dinner was great. I knew a handful of people there oddly enough—they were a bunch of Tom's friends.

Once dinner was over the group split. Jeremy and I stayed in the back of the room. He kissed me and said, "I've been wanting to do that for a while now." We left and went to Tenjune (where we met). The cab ride was a great mix of good conversation and good (great) kissing. At Tenjune we danced, we shouted, we drank, we smiled a lot. While we were dancing he said, "I don't want to take up your whole weekend, but I'm having a party tomorrow night and would love for you to come." I melted. My Saturday was secure. We left shortly after that and walked hand in hand to his place.

The sex was long and hard—he is so much man for me to wrap myself around. We undressed each other. I went down on him then climbed on top. We went back and forth between me on top then him on top. When I'm on top and he decides he wants to be on top he lifts me and stands up—stays inside me the whole time—we have sex in mid air for a few seconds and then he lays me back down and continues to fuck me with his brand of fervor. This I love. He kept checking in with me. He'd kiss me and say, "Hi," or he'd say, "Hi," first then kiss me. It lasted a while . . . some 45 minutes. I wasn't sure if he came. Afterward we fell asleep for a little bit (long enough for me to learn that he snores ☺) and then we woke up and did it again. That time I was sure he came. He held me through the night and there was lots of bad breath kissing in the morning (neither of us seemed to mind).

The morning sex was unreal—we had adjusted to each other's bodies. The first time he came, after a while of rolling around, he kneeled and pulled my hips to his (I stayed lying down). He came all over me (at my breathless request). It was messy and beautiful. The second time I was on top—I hadn't been there for very long. We just hit our stride and it felt incredible. I love looking at him when I'm on top. He's a gorgeous sight to see, and his face gives away his pleasure so easily. We actually look at each other—I've found that someone's eyes are usually closed in this position. He always licks his thumb and rubs my clit, which intensifies the already very intense. Afterward he holds on to me so tightly. Like he loves me . . . or at least like he's willing to love me.

April 12, 2007

I spent another (wonderful) night with Jeremy. We went to a dinner party in a gorgeous apartment in SoHo. During dinner he and I had a poignant conversation—he told me a very sad story about a friend of his from college. When we got back to his place we drank red wine and talked in the living room for a while. Later he went down on me for the first time. He stopped in the middle and I was afraid it was because he didn't like doing it, but he came up and told me he needed positive reinforcement (was cute)—so I moaned and groaned until I came (lasted about 8 seconds). We spent the next day together—sex, breakfast, movie (*Back to the Future*), sex, another movie (*Shawshank Redemption*). I forget which time (think it was the first) we ended up fucking at the end of his bed. He was sitting up and I was on top. I looked over my left shoulder and enjoyed the view from the full-length mirror leaning against the wall.

    I didn't hear from him after that :(By Wednesday it had been five days and I gave up. Of course it didn't make sense, but I'm too old for it to have to make sense. When together I feel like his angel when apart I'm out of his mind. I did write him an e-mail that I never sent and I concocted a clever (or so I thought) text message that I had planned to send on Tuesday (I didn't pick that day for any reason.) I decided not to send it, which felt good. Then that Tuesday he did call. It was almost 11 and I was just getting into bed. I didn't answer because I couldn't pretend everything was okay but I was also in no position, nor did I want to, bite his head off. I was glad he called though because it gave me a platform to write him and end things on the up and up.

In my journal there isn't much transition between good and bad. What happened was, I left his apartment on Saturday evening and jumped in a cab. I texted him from there (I didn't write this exchange down, I just remember it). **Me:** *It's very cold . . . memories of you and your bed will keep me warm.* **Him:** *Aww, baby :) I'll be thinking of my cowgirl all day.* That cowgirl thing is kind of embarrassing. *C'est la vie.* After that, the days came and the call from him didn't. I knew if we were going to continue, I'd have heard from him by Monday. Rereading my journal now, I see that allowing five days was generous, but it's that blasted benefit of the doubt that I'll willingly extend to a man whose smile temporarily rules my world. Regardless, his silence came in loud and clear.

I was tempted to send him an e-mail saying something along the lines of "You're not interested. I get it. But if we run into each other, things don't have to be awkward." I can't adequately explain the social networking of this, but each time I visit New York, which is regularly, the odds of my running into him are decent. He was one person I really didn't want to be weird around, but I still didn't feel that that gave me license to write him. Then he called. Ten days later. I knew the point of resolute interest on his part had come and gone, but I did listen to his voice mail and very much enjoyed the sweet, sexy sound of not being blown off completely. I am a closure aficionada and this opened the door for me to write him.

Wednesday, April 18, 2007, 5:08 P.M.

Hey, Handsome,

Thanks for calling—was good to hear your voice. The reason I am (rudely) responding with an e-mail instead of a call is because it's easier for me to say what I need to here. Otherwise I'm sure I'd be distracted by your southern drawl (which totally comes out over the phone :) and would just want to have steamy phone sex. I'm assuming (a dangerous thing to do, I know) that based on the time it took you to get back in touch that you probably want this to be more casual than I do. Unfortunately ;) I'm crazy about you and wouldn't be able to keep up casual pretenses for very long.

I am, however, very much looking forward to the friendship portion of our program. I'll surely see you at obnoxious clubs and sophisticated dinner parties alike, and I'll be here next time you're in town visiting the Wharton boys. Thank you again and again for three wonderful weekends.

Samara

Friday, April 20, 2007, 3:06 P.M.
Hey, Sexy—

I'm sorry I haven't gotten back to you yet but this week has been crazy and I have to cancel my weekend plans and travel for work this afternoon. Joy. Thanks for the e-mail and I just wanted you to know that I have more to say but probably won't be able to clear my head for a couple days. Even if I haven't gotten it on the page yet I hope you know that I do think about you. Have a good weekend and I'll be in touch.

Jeremy

Of course, I didn't know he thought about me—all evidence pointed directly to the contrary. That one sentence was my only proof, and so I read it seventeen times. His follow-up to this e-mail never came, and I had a feeling it wouldn't. As I mentioned, however, the odds of running into him were on the very possible side, and a month later I did. Chloé and I went to a Tuesday-night birthday party. We came in late and were there for about thirty-five minutes. It was long enough for me to relax and know he wasn't coming. Then he walked in. My stomach fell to the floor. I was going to pick it up but thought that might draw too much attention, so I just kicked it behind a potted plant. In my experience, men do one of two things in these situations. They (1) completely ignore you or (2) pretend it never happened. Jeremy walked directly into our circle. He kissed me on the cheek and said, "How are you, stranger?" Right, because it's my fault we've been out of touch. It looked like we were going with option 2, which wasn't ideal but was decidedly better than option 1.

Jeremy and I ended up on separate sides of the room for a while but came back together within the hour. Later he suggested we go somewhere we could talk. We found a less boisterous bar nearby. We caught up a bit, and then all of a sudden an unsolicited apology entered stage left. It was long and difficult for me to listen to, mainly because I'm one who tends to put my hands in the surrender position and say, "Oh, no, no, don't worry about it." I was giving myself strict instructions not to do that this time. *He owes you an apology; now shut up and listen to it.*

Now, I know what you're thinking. Chloé shouted it at me the next day. I said, "He apologized." She snapped, "He apologized because he wanted to get laid!" I'm not saying sex didn't cross Jeremy's mind—in fact, I know it did. I am saying that I know exactly what a man asking me to go home with him for the twelfth time looks like, and this was not that. Jeremy apologized, and I thanked him. We continued talking. He didn't suggest we leave. He didn't suggest showing me just how sorry he was. He didn't temporarily profess wanting to be exclusive just so I'd go home with him. We conversed about things both interesting and arbitrary. I was the one who finally said, "It's three a.m. and you have to work tomorrow."

When all was said and done, Chloé never boasted, "I told you so." She simply said how sorry she was, and then she asked me how I felt. I said I wouldn't trade it for anything. His apology made me feel like everything that was said and done wasn't for naught. For skepticism's sake, however, and, more importantly, for Chloé's savvy sake, I won't rule out the possibility that it was a game from the get-go and Jeremy picked me up and played me like a fiddle. Except for one thing: I am not a fiddle. I am a slender, sophisticated, intricate violin—a Stradivarius if you really want to get specific. It is an instrument an expert wouldn't touch unless he planned on playing with precision.

In Retrospect

Having sex and writing about having sex are two different things. They are undoubtedly related but still very different. One requires you to be uninhibited and extroverted, while the other calls for being alone and introspective. They can both, however, feel absolutely incredible, and writing about sex makes it last that much longer. It gives you further insight into the overall experience and also into yourself as a sexual creature. Writing about this circumstance taught me not only about my updated desires and the chemistry I have with this one man in particular, but also that I should stand by my decisions no matter what the outcome. Nothing here felt wrong to me and therefore it wasn't. In the past, if a man had not gotten back to me after being notably affectionate and saying many kind things, I would have thought I did something wrong. Not this time.

In the end, Jeremy's tendency to treat me like a Victoria's Secret Angel when I was directly in front of him and like the first contestant eliminated from *America's Next Top Model* when I wasn't obviously didn't make him my next great love. It did, however, make him my long-awaited—um, well-deserved, if I do say so myself—lover, in every sense of the sultry word. He was sent into my world to remind me that I can desire and be desired at all hours of the day. That I can lose myself in someone without losing my mind. That I can say yes when I want to and no when I have to. That sex is the most important meal of the day. That I can handle being played—provided the violinist holds his instrument properly and knows the music very well.

ANAÏS NIN (1903–1977) ON SEX
BOTH GOOD AND BAD

Anaïs Nin was born Angela Anaïs Juana Antolina Rosa Edelmira Nin y Culmell in France in 1903 and became one of the first females to write well-known erotic short stories. Her father, Joaquin Nin, deserted her, her mother, and her two brothers when she was eleven years old. Her mother moved the family to New York City, where Anaïs, after dropping out of school at the age of sixteen, worked as a model and a dancer. Just after her father left, Anaïs began writing in a diary. It proved to be her ultimate companion, as she continued to write in it until just before her death. The diary also went on to become her most acclaimed work—it's been published in twelve volumes.

At twenty, Anaïs married banker Hugh Guiler and moved to Paris. While living in the City of Lights, she met her muse: writer Henry Miller. The affair, which included Henry's wife, June, was first detailed in the book *Henry and June* and continues in *Incest: From "A Journal of Love": The Unexpurgated Diary of Anaïs Nin* (from where the following two excerpts are taken). This volume of the diary entails Anaïs's bohemian lifestyle in Paris as well as her sexual adventures with Miller, her psychoanalyst René Allendy, and (brace yourself) her father. At the suggestion of another therapist, Otto Rank (who she also had a tryst with), she beds her father, then dumps him as punishment for abandoning her when she was young.

Her accounts with each of these men are written in gripping prose. She once wrote, "I'm going to write the absolute truth in my journal because reality deserves to be described in the vilest terms." Anaïs has an engaging way of recounting the intellectual and emotional aspects of the sexual experience along with the physical act itself. I wish I had room for more of these excerpts. Alas, I can only include two. The first is a satisfying encounter with Miller and the second an unsettling rendezvous with Allendy, in which she ends up comparing Allendy to Miller. She compares most of her lovers to Miller.

March 25, 1933

Henry came and laughed away my black mood. Said he felt so innocent of any disloyalty. I said, "You are only true to the impulse of the moment. I cheat and play tricks, but you remain at the center—immovable." He was tender and truly irresponsible. Laughed because he said I understood the big liberties and tripped over the small obstacles. . . .

We laugh. We lie together, fucking softly, gently, swimming in it, and for the first time the orgasm comes to me unsought, peacefully almost, like a slow dawn, a slow flowering out of relaxation and yieldingness and nonbeing. No reaching out for it. Falling like rain, flowering, drowning the mind. . . .

April 19, 1933

Métro Cadet. I'm late and Allendy thought I was not coming. Experience, curiosity, comedy. But I would like some whiskey. Allendy doesn't like my wanting whiskey. He says he never takes anything to drink in the afternoon and so he won't now, it would upset his habits. When he says this I drink more fiercely. It's humorous. Allons doncs. The French room, in blue now. Shutters closed. Lugubrious. Lanterns and velvet. The alcove. As in eighteenth-century engravings! The beard and the French and all! The alcove.

Allendy doesn't kiss me. He sits on the edge of the bed and says, "Now you will pay for everything, for enslaving me and then abandoning me. Petite garce!"

And he takes a whip out of his pocket!

Now, I had not counted on the whip. I didn't know how to regard it. I was enjoying Allendy's fierceness—the fantastic eyes, his anger, the will in him.

He ordered that I should undress. I undressed slowly. . . .

As I write all this I recognize the dime-novel quality of it. If I had read more cheap novels I might have recognized it immediately, but I only know them by hearsay.

Experience. Curiosity. Coldness. I don't know yet how to treat that whip. When Allendy tries a few preliminary lashes I'm simply angry and feel like hitting back. I don't yet see any "voluptuous" quality in it. In fact, I'm laughing. My pride is gravely offended. It seems to me this is like my Father beating me. I feel I ought to be cute and charming so he will be disarmed.

I had been fighting off Allendy's blows and decided to take my chemise off to affect him. At the same time, I provoked his fury by saying, "No, I don't want it. You can't do that."

"I'll reduce you to a rag," said Allendy. "You will crawl and do everything I bid you. I want you to abdicate—forget your pride—forget everything."

"I won't."

"You can't help it. You can scream. Nobody pays any attention to screams in this house."

"I don't want it because the marks will show. I don't want Hugo to see them, nor Henry either!"

At this Allendy laid me on the bed and whipped my buttocks, hard.

But I noticed this: His penis, after all this excitement on his part—lashes, struggles, caresses of fury, kisses on the breasts—was still soft. Henry would have already been blazing. Allendy pushed my head toward it, as the first time, and then, with all the halo of excitement, threats, he fucked no better than before. His penis was short and nerveless. Voluptuary! He found it. I played a comedy. Allendy said he had reached the height of joy. He lay panting and satisfied.

ENDNOTES:

THIS ABOVE ALL

Peace. It does not mean to be in a place where there is
no noise, trouble, or hard work. It means to be in the midst
of these things·and still be calm in your heart.

—Unknown

(Copied into my journal on July 6, 2004)

For our final pages together, I'm going to reiterate one of the earliest lessons we ever learned: Don't lie. It's amazing how naturally lying comes to us, isn't it? No one ever has to teach us. We spill juice on the carpet and Mommy says, "Did you do that?" And then it hits us, *Oh, I know. I'll just tell her I didn't do it! She'll be none the wiser.* But she is, of course, the wiser, and she shouts vehemently at us not to lie anymore. And then our teachers tell us not to lie. Then our friends say it's okay to lie to the authorities but not to lie to them. Then in every romantic relationship we choose to indulge, it'll be stated over and over, "Be honest! Just tell me how you really feel." It's strange, though, that amidst all those "don't lie" lessons, no one ever tells you the one person you *will* end up lying to the most often and the one person you *really* shouldn't be lying to at all is yourself.

You'll tell yourself you like a job when you don't. You'll tell yourself you're in love with someone when you aren't. You'll tell yourself you aren't attracted to a person when you are. You'll tell yourself you don't really want to go after that dream job for reasons *a, b,* and *c,* but in truth you put it off because you're terrified. Basically, it's because that dream job and that new relationship would be too tough. Too complicated. You'll stick with your current job and an uninspired relationship because they're easy. They're convenient.

I've decided recently that our days aren't meant to be convenient. If you wake up and find that your life is really convenient, I suggest running (not walking) to the next challenge. Life is meant to be rewarding, and reward only comes from hard work that you want to be doing. The work can be physical, mental, or emotional. It can entail an occupation, a relationship, or a project such as building your son a tree house. You have to find those things that are worthy of your pursuit, and it starts by being honest with yourself. Pull out your journal and be brutally, painfully, overwhelmingly, and cathartically honest with yourself. You don't have to start being that honest with everyone else just yet, but you will find in being honest with yourself, it comes much more naturally to be honest and kind to others.

In the countless quiet hours I've spent with my journal, I have recorded moments both simple and emotionally inundating; I have scratched wounds wide open in order to start the healing process; I have recorded my vices with a trembling hand and laughed out loud at them later; I have identified some of my more glaring flaws with the hope of correcting them; I have inspired, embarrased, and stunned myself; I found the career I want to have and the woman I want to be and have started working diligently toward those goals. My journal has been my confidant and poor man's therapist for over twelve years now. I feel as though I have made substantial progress as a person: I am not nearly as jealous as I once was. I am no longer tormented by my intellectual shortcomings but rather familiar and comfortable with what I am and am not capable of. I find every age is better than the one before, and I no longer hate being tall, which I did for the first twenty years of my life.

I still have plenty of work to do. I am far too judgmental. I need to learn how to apologize to people in person and admit I'm wrong sooner than later. I also need to teach myself how to give constructive criticism and not tell others what I think they want to hear. My sister tells me I need to stop sticking my fingers in the pancake batter, but I'm not sure about that one yet. There's time to attempt these improvements, and I look forward to the introspective road ahead as well as the many mistakes I'll make along the way. I plan to observe, enjoy, criticize, taste, touch, and smell the world around me and document it all in notes to myself. I highly recommend you do the same. It is remarkable how much inner strength one can actually summon.

FOR YOUR READING PLEASURE

A Few Favorite Characters Who Have Come to Similar Conclusions About the Importance of Self in Relationship to Others

- As the Cady Heron (Lindsay Lohan) Voice-Over Said During the Math Competition in the Film Mean Girls: *"Calling somebody else fat won't make you any skinnier. Calling someone stupid doesn't make you any smarter. And ruining Regina George's life definitely didn't make me any happier. All you can do in life is try to solve the problem in front of you."*

- As Carrie Bradshaw (Sarah Jessica Parker) Said in Her Final Voice-Over in the Series Finale of Sex and the City: *". . . the most exciting, challenging, and significant relationship of all is the one you have with yourself. And if you can find someone to love the you you love, well, that's just fabulous."*

- And Finally, as William Shakespeare Wrote in his Acclaimed Tragedy *Hamlet* and as the Characters Cher (Alicia Silverstone) and Heather (Susan Mohun) Reiterated in the Car in the Movie *Clueless: "This above all: To thine own self be true, and it must follow, as the night the day, thou canst not then be false to any man."*

ACKNOWLEDGMENTS

ADAM CHROMY (AGENT PROVOCATEUR): I believe you had issues with your placement in the last book. Well, I'm giving you the top spot this time around because you rock my world on a regular basis. Not that you didn't back then—you just do it more often now. It is a distinct pleasure to continue working with someone who is doing exactly what he was born to do. I am the grateful beneficiary of your persistence, wit, and wisdom.

GOD ALMIGHTY (THE ONE WHO CREATES AND RESTORES EVERY-THING THERE IS): My friend Frank always used to say, "I *know* God has a sense of humor. Have you *ever* seen a platypus?" It is your sense of humor I count on now more than ever. Thank you for laughter, love, understanding, and rainbows after really loud storms. Thank you also for the gift of words and the unlimited order in which they can be placed.

ANNE COLE (EDITOR EXTRAORDINAIRE): I know for sure that you have a sense of humor, and you completely understand why I had to put Adam and God first. Once again, working with you is one pleasure after another. Congratulations (in print) on your promotion—if you don't mind, I'm just going to hang on while you keep working your way up. Thank you for sharing my vision with me and for holding your lantern high and keeping us on the straight and narrow.

KIMBERLY COWSER (PUBLICIST AFTER MY OWN HEART): It's not the amount of work you do that amazes me, as much as the fact that you do it all with a smile on your face. I don't know what I did to end up with a live wire like you on my team, but I'm gonna keep doing it. Thank you for sharing your creativity, attentiveness, and overwhelming kindness with me so readily.

JESSE JOYCE (FUNNY GUY): I guess I'm going to have to keep including you in my books just so I can get you to read them. Thank you for looking over anything and everything I throw at you and for calling me at 2:13 A.M. to tell me what you think. I am forever grateful for your enthusiasm and friendship.

RICHARD CLARK (LITERARY SCHOLAR): And what would this tome be without you, my good friend? It would be minus Samuel Pepys and *Moby Dick; or, The Whale* (not to mention that that title would have been punctuated incorrectly.) Thank you for taking all of my random questions so seriously and for reading my work so thoroughly. In case I haven't said it yet, it's great to be back in touch.

THOMAS DEVANEY (POET LAUREATE): Missing a train has never worked out so well for me. Truth be told, I almost gave up on poetry, but you re-endeared me to the art. Thank you for that and also for telling me all about William James and his journal. I very much look forward to your next book—I'll sign yours if you sign mine!

MOM AND DAD (PARENTS): There are many things parents should not know about their children. Most of those things are in this book. Thank you for your support with no ceiling and your love with no limits. You are my sunshine.

SOURCES

Frank, Anne. *The Diary of a Young Girl: The Definitive Edition*. Edited by Otto H. Frank and Mirjam Pressler. Translated by Susan Massotty. New York: Doubleday, 1995.

Green, Roger Lancelyn, ed. *The Diaries of Lewis Carroll, Vol. 1*. New York: Oxford University Press, 1954.

Kukil, Karen V., ed. *The Unabridged Journals of Sylvia Plath*. New York: Anchor Books, 2000.

Le Gallienne, Richard, ed. *The Diary of Samuel Pepys*. New York: The Modern Library, 2003.

Miller, Randall A., and Linda Patterson Miller, eds. *The Book of American Diaries*. New York: Avon Books, 1995. (Source of the John Wilkes Booth journal entry.)

Nin, Anaïs. *Incest: From "A Journal of Love."* New York: Harcourt, 1992.

Oates, Joyce Carol. *The Journal of Joyce Carol Oates: 1973–1982*. New York: Ecco, 2007.

Paine, Thomas. *Common Sense*. New York: Prometheus Books, 1995.

Stern, Madeleine B., Joel Myerson, and Daniel Shealy, eds. *The Journals of Louisa May Alcott*. Athens: University of Georgia Press, 1997.

Williams, Tennessee. *Notebooks*. Edited by Margaret Bradham Thornton. New Haven: Yale University Press, 2006.